"Finding the Flow is a helpful book written by two practitioners who have lived and breathed small groups in their local church. This book will help every current or prospective leader of small groups be more effective. This is must-reading for small group leaders!"
Jim Tomberlin, founder, Third Quarter Consulting, and former regional pastor, Willow Creek Community Church

"Here is the total package! If you lead a small group or oversee a small groups ministry of any kind, you need this book, especially if you're bored with the old 'tried and true' methods. Here is a guide for growing groups in this postmodern era. The authors—who write engagingly and with uncommon transparency, wisdom and grace—provide readers all they need to make small groups successful. They show how groups can be God's mechanism for profound spiritual transformation. The section on helping group leaders understand themselves before they facilitate groups is worth the price of the book. . . . After reading a few pages, you will wish that you were in a group that Jenn and Tara were coleading."
William W. Klein, professor of New Testament, Denver Seminary

"Practical yet profound. *Finding the Flow* is a necessary companion for anyone involved in small group leadership and development."
Robert E. Logan, president, CoachNet International

"Community doesn't come with a manual. But if it's experience and wisdom you're looking for, Miller and Peppers have a ton of it. Using real-life examples, solid relationship principles and hands-on exercises, *Finding the Flow* explores the dynamics of gatherings that thrive versus survive, and the facilitation practices that can help make the difference."
Sally Morgenthaler, contributor to *An Emergent Manifesto of Hope*

"This is one of the most practical books available regarding how to develop transformational leaders who can in turn lead transformational groups. What sets their work apart from all the other small group books out there is their focus on the leader of the group. I've seen Jenn and Tara at work firsthand in the church where I pastor, and they've taken the small group ministry to a new level of effectiveness."
Ron Johnson, founding and lead pastor, Pathways Church, Denver, Colorado

"An interactive, conversational and engaging guide to empower and equip group leaders, helping them create life-changing environments that produce passionate followers of Christ."
Bill Donahue, pastor of leadership development, Willow Creek Community Church, and author of *Leading Life-Changing Small Groups*

A Guide for Leading Small Groups and Gatherings

FINDING THE FLOW

Tara Miller and Jenn Peppers

Foreword by Joseph Myers

IVP Connect

An imprint of InterVarsity Press
Downers Grove, Illinois

InterVarsity Press
P.O. Box 1400, Downers Grove, IL 60515-1426
World Wide Web: www.ivpress.com
E-mail: email@ivpress.com

InterVarsity Press® is the book-publishing division of InterVarsity Christian Fellowship/USA®, a student movement active on campus at hundreds of universities, colleges and schools of nursing in the United States of America, and a member movement of the International Fellowship of Evangelical Students. For information about local and regional activities, write Public Relations Dept., InterVarsity Christian Fellowship/USA, 6400 Schroeder Rd., P.O. Box 7895, Madison, WI 53707-7895, or visit the IVCF website at <www.intervarsity.org>.

All Scripture quotations, unless otherwise indicated, are taken from the Holy Bible, Today's New International Version™ Copyright © 2001 by International Bible Society. All rights reserved.

Design: Cindy Kiple

Images: Leigh Schindler/Getty Images

ISBN 978-0-8308-1094-9

Printed in the United States of America ∞

 InterVarsity Press is committed to protecting the environment and to the responsible use of natural resources. As a member of Green Press Initiative we use recycled paper whenever possible. To learn more about the Green Press Initiative, visit <www.greenpressinitiative.org>.

Library of Congress Cataloging-in-Publication Data

Miller, Tara, 1971-
  Finding the flow: a guide for small group facilitators/Tara
  Miller and Jenn Peppers.
    p. cm
  Includes bibliographical references.
  ISBN 978-0-8308-1094-9 (pbk.: alk. paper)
  1. Church group work. 2. Small groups—Religious
  aspects—Christianity. I. Peppers, Jenn, 1968- II. Title.
  BV652.2.M495 2008
  253'.7—dc22

                   2008031402

P	21	20	19	18	17	16	15	14	13	12	11	10	9	8	7	6	5	4	3	2	1
Y	26	25	24	23	22	21	20	19	18	17	16	15	14	13	12	11	10	09	08		

To Mark and Sammy, of course.

To Sammy: An amazing husband and loving friend.
Your support of our endeavor was invaluable.
Thank you for the sacrifices you made that helped
bring our vision to life.

To Mark: My partner in life and ministry.
You've been with me through virtually all of the stories in this book
and we've learned so much from each other along the way.
Thanks for being by my side through it all.

CONTENTS

FOREWORD

Almost every week you can find me down at your local blues club. It might surprise some of you that I'm a blues performer and guitarist. Blues is where I find home. I love the blues. I love the music, the soul, the people, and I like the predictably of each unique song.

Most every blues song weaves its way through a twelve-bar series of music using a chord progression that is predictable and yet unique to every song. Blues has a musical pattern. Blues *is* a musical pattern. It is this pattern that helps the music find a "bluesy" flow and sets it apart from other genres of music.

You might think that a genre of music would have a short lifespan if it primarily were scored around twelve bars of music and only three chords. But you'd be wrong. There are thousands of blues songs that use this pattern all in their unique way . . . and not only blues songs. This pattern has influenced everything from rock to gospel, country to pop. Yet each song stands alone, finding its unique way to flow into someone's soul.

Blues is not the only thing that uses predictably unique patterns in this way. I received two photos from two different people. One was a close-up of a rosebud and the other was taken from the *Hubble* scope of a new universe forming. When put side by side, the contents of the photos were shaped with similar patterns. Celebrated architect Christopher Alexander would say that all beauty looks the same because it flows from the same patterns . . . rose and universe.

Artists have known for years that a person's face is formed around a pattern of fourths and fifths. And yet each persons face is unique to them. To categorize species we use these predictably unique patterns, and yet there are no two in a species that are exactly the same. There are patterns everywhere, and each pattern is used in a predictably unique way.

This is the key genius of *Finding the Flow*. People use patterns of connection. *Finding the Flow* helps leaders spot these patterns and maneuver through them in a way that's not prescriptive. *Finding the Flow* describes many of the patterns people use as they connect and then gives the leader practical ways to navigate without getting lost in a controlling vortex.

This is a field book for spotting the patterns people use to connect. This is not a guide to clone groups. This is a guide to help you develop environments where people can connect in organically ordered patterns. You will find help with patterns of behavior, personality, connection and health. To try and use the contents as a prescriptive "way" of forming small groupings would only lead you into deeper frustration. There is no prescribed way. However, there are patterns that can be described, and they will benefit the leader when applied in predictably unique forms.

So head into your next grouping with this field book under your arm so you can more naturally find your flow and the flow of the group without building a dam to stop the current. Feel free to find your natural and unique flow, and free others to do likewise.

Joseph Myers
Author of *The Search to Belong* and *Organic Community*

ACKNOWLEDGMENTS

Special thanks to Pathways Church in Denver (www.pathwayschurch .org), and Ron Johnson, its lead pastor, for creating a ministry environment that gave both of us the opportunity to develop our gifts, be challenged, make mistakes, try again and grow.

Thank you, Sally Morgenthaler (www.trueconversations.com), for your enthusiasm about our project and for your part in paving the way for other female authors and leaders.

Thank you to the many pastors and small group facilitators who took time to meet with us to share their hearts and stories. Thanks to all of those who have led groups we've been a part of and helped us learn and let us use their stories. And thanks to all those facilitators at Pathways who have faithfully led groups and opened their homes.

JENN

MY JOURNEY HAS BEEN POSSIBLE BECAUSE OF the family, friends and leaders who believed in me and observed what I could not see. They have helped me to overcome obstacles and view myself through the eyes of Jesus in ways that have been redeeming and transforming.

Thank you to my immediate family and in-laws for their deep love for me and for each other. Love covers a multitude of sins.

Thanks to my dearest friends and small group for support, encouragement and ideas along the way: Debbie Wallace, Kristen Hattlestad, Beth Mann, Carole Buglewicz, Cara Silva, Jodi and Todd Horner, Brooke and David Craven, and Sarah and Thomas Goodwin.

There are many leaders who have had a tremendous influence on me, either directly or indirectly, but I feel especially grateful for those involved in conversations I consider transformational. Many thanks to Tim Pynes for his spiritual direction, Bev Powers for her guidance and counsel, and my friends at WayPoint Coaching Community.

And thank you, Tara Miller, an incredible partner, inspiration and friend. You are an amazing writer, and I am honored to work with you.

TARA

THANKS TO MY FAMILY AND ESPECIALLY my two beautiful daughters, Chloe and Raina. I love you very, very much.

Thanks to Bob Logan, who believed in me and left the door open. I learned most of what I know about leadership development from you, and I have barely scratched the surface. Your work coaching ministry leaders continues to yield eternal dividends.

Thanks to Steve Logan, my supervisor/coach, who walked alongside me as I learned what it meant to be a small groups pastor. Your gifts of encouragement, perspective and patience were much needed and much appreciated.

Thanks to Harv Powers, a mentor and friend, who saw me through some of my darkest times. Your ability to see when no one else can is remarkable. Your influence on me and your model of redemptive leadership can be felt throughout this book.

Thanks to my friends for support and encouragement along the way: Nancy Hightower, Chad and Susanne Klawetter, John and Hillary Stark, Bill and Phyllis Klein, Brad and Debbie Ellgen, Brad and Louise Richey, Jeannette Slater, Dave and Natalie Huff, and Lori Rogers.

And thanks to Jenn Peppers, who I quite literally could not have done this without! You've been amazing to work with, as well as a great friend.

INTRODUCTION

This is what the LORD says:
"Let not the wise boast of their wisdom
or the strong boast of their strength
or the rich boast of their riches,
but let those who boast boast about this:
that they understand and know me,
that I am the LORD, who exercises kindness,
justice and righteousness on earth,
for in these I delight,"
declares the LORD.

JEREMIAH 9:23-24

We didn't start out to write a book. What we were actually doing was developing a training program for the small group leaders in our church. Somewhere along the way, we realized we had a philosophy about the types of group experiences that lead to encounters with God, and also about how to engage with Scripture in a way that affects how we live. It seemed like something was forming that was cohesive and coherent—at least most of the time. Maybe this could actually be helpful for other churches, we thought. At that point the whole thing morphed into a book.

We should probably start by introducing ourselves. In fact, throughout the book, we'll be sharing some thoughts from each of us individually. We share our stories because people learn through stories, just like the disciples learned through the stories Jesus told. But we also share them because that's what we want groups to do. After all, groups—whether they are small groups, community groups, missional groups or house churches—are about people, about their stories and about how God enters into those stories.

TARA

I was a small groups pastor at a church in Denver, a church that could be loosely termed nontraditional. And I was looking for a way to train and resource our small group facilitators. We had some great natural leaders, people who lead in the business world or are teachers and medical professionals. But many of them, not having been raised in any type of faith system, had never facilitated small groups in a church setting before.

I'm sure that over time they would have figured out their own methods that worked for them, how to avoid common pitfalls, things to look for, what they were really shooting for in a group. By and large, they're extremely bright, capable people. But anytime you can avoid some trial-and-error learning (no one can avoid all of it) and help facilitators feel supported by and connected with each other at the same time, it's a good thing. Why learn from your own mistakes when you can learn at least some things from other people's mistakes?

But I needed a way to train them that wouldn't feel like prepackaged church training. Everything I looked at felt like it wasn't written for us—it didn't have us in mind. Much of it used a liberal amount of Christianese, which half of our people don't understand and sends the other half running for the door when they hear it. Most of the books and training materials I looked at had good principles, but I could see the huge amount of translation I'd be required to do to make it communicate to our people.

JENN

I DIDN'T BECOME A FOLLOWER OF CHRIST until my late twenties and have "grown up" in small yet growing nondenominational churches. As such, I've had limited exposure to church programs and curricula. Most of my adult career has been in the corporate world, and so most of the training I've experienced and created was in that context. A few years ago I also began doing some seminar-style trainings at our church, where I'm an elder—first coaching training, then a series of seminars on career transition. I naturally borrowed the corporate style for these events, since that's what I'm most familiar with. I was surprised at one of the most common responses I got: "What's great about this is that I can use this material not only in church but also in my career, my family and my relationships. It's so versatile!" I realized that many of the church trainings people had attended in the past were limited to that sphere only and didn't feel as integrated into the rest of life, which spiritual things were designed to be. I felt that kind of compartmentalization could interfere with the potential for a more holistic spirituality.

I wanted to experiment with this idea further, so I called Tara to suggest that we create some kind of training or equipping system that would help small group facilitators. I've been involved in small groups since I started attending church and have experienced the essential role they play in spiritual growth and community. I also met my husband, Sammy, in a small group. So it's an area that's close to my heart. But I knew we'd need something different from what was helpful for more traditional churches.

○   ○   ○

For the rest to make sense, you'll probably need to know a little more about the people in our congregation and the perspectives we hold. And there may be a spark of recognition for you in the description. Our church specializes in being unchurchy. We actually work quite hard to be unconventional, sometimes even in cases where the conventional was working just fine. Most people at our church were either not brought up in church or didn't have, shall we say, the most positive church experiences growing up. You won't hear a lot of Christianese. You will hear a mix of cynicism and enthusiasm that isn't always consistent. Most people come casual, and once in a while someone will even show up barefoot (this is Colorado, after all). Although in recent years we've attracted a broader age range of people, the average age is still around thirty. For every tattoo, you'll see a minivan with cartoon-character sunshades—that's the bridge we're crossing. And we're mighty conflicted about it.

THE LANGUAGE BARRIER

We are much more apt to describe ourselves by the things that we aren't than by the things that we are. In fact, language presents a continuing problem. When we can't stand the current terminology anymore, we find new ways to say old things. (Which is what has always been done—otherwise we'd be writing to you in Shakespearian English or, better yet, Old Anglo-Saxon.) Certain words can't be used, such as *program* (too bureaucratic), *backslider* (too fundamentalist), or *Gen-X* (way too last-decade).

In the creation of our training material, we made the decision to change from *leader* to *facilitator* because we realized many people react negatively to that term. They'd rather "help" than "lead." Regardless of the term any of us use, the facilitator does have certain leadership responsibilities. Yet we've found that to many people, *lead* has too much of a one-up, one-down connotation, as if one person is above another. Many feel too inexperienced, too unspiritual or too uneducated to lead others. Being labeled a leader doesn't fly well in a culture raised on egalitarianism and equality. Everyone's thoughts are just as valid as everyone else's, so who are we to pretend to know more? *Leading* begins to sound too much like arrogance. So no one takes the lead. Which feels like a relief to most of us, really. After all, how often have we followed the wrong leader? Or seen leaders *fall?* (Another word we don't generally use in less-than-traditional church culture.)

Given this language barrier, there may be some terms used here that will not work in your church either. Perhaps the term *small groups* conjures memories of church-imposed community where everyone was marching in lock-step or maybe of judgmentalism disguised as accountability. For this reason, many church small group ministries have rechristened themselves as community groups, life groups, transformation groups, home groups or something similar. But for the sake of simplicity we've decided to stick with the term *small groups*, hoping the majority of readers will be okay with that.

And really, we focus more on skills than forms of group life. Whether you're part of a house church, a missional church, a traditional church or a megachurch, these same skills for facilitating group life will be essential.

We believe that there is really nothing new under the sun as far as language goes, just new ways of saying old things. But we also knew that we needed material that could be presented to our facilitators without immediately being labeled as ineffective or outdated due to the language or packaging. Also, given the resistance in many churches to standard programs, we decided not to create a program but rather to equip people with skills that are valuable and timeless regardless of the purpose or format of the group.

The more we explored the idea, the more we felt drawn to create opportunities for group facilitators to get in sync with the Spirit of God and find the "flow." Since both of us have been in groups and led groups, we know that effective group facilitation involves listening to and following the Spirit. One of the main purposes of this book is to help address common obstacles so facilitators can follow the Spirit more effectively and freely. By removing obstacles, facilitators will be more present, less likely to get stuck and more likely to ask where God is in the present situation.

We also need to make the brief disclaimer that we're not writing this because we know everything and have it all figured out. On the contrary—we definitely don't. We've seen things done well and not so well, and we've done things both well and not so well. Most of our experience and qualifications come from having done things poorly and learned from those mistakes. So know that we're still exploring and learning as we write this.

But before we describe more about how we've gone about equipping small group facilitators, it will probably be helpful for you to have a better understanding of our perspective on the church (as in the church universal, the body of Christ) as a whole. Small groups serve as a microcosm of the larger church, highlighting its pluses and minuses.

THE CHURCH IS MESSED UP

How's that for a subhead that gives it all away? The problem with the church, as has been observed many times, is that it's full of sinners. Some horrible things have happened in churches. We've all had bad church experiences and have likely caused some bad church experiences for other people along the way. So we get mad, leave our local church, try to find a better one—or maybe don't try. It happens all the time. A late medieval manuscript says, "The church is something like Noah's ark. If it weren't for the storm outside, [we] couldn't stand the smell inside." It was true then, and it's still true today.

Most of us have a general idea of the flaws of the church, but according to recent research by George Barna, popularized in his book *The Revolution*, it appears we may be even worse off than we thought. Willow Creek Community Church drew similar conclusions in its research project "Reveal." The church is spending tons of money on real estate and renovations and staff and programs, but is it radically changing society? Or people? The conclusion of these research projects is, not really. Infidelities, pornography, addictions, hunger for power and so forth are as rampant inside the church as outside. Charitable giving is a little higher, but the gap is closing. "Reveal" concluded that to experience true transformation, the most important factor is simply that a person take personal responsibility for his or her own spiritual growth. That's a quality often hard to come by in many churches.

It seems that hardly a day goes by that we don't hear someone take a shot at Christians, the church or faith. Whether the source is a news story, a conversation with a stranger, a movie or a magazine article, it seems ubiquitous. And admittedly, it has become pretty easy to take issue with the church. As P. J. O'Rourke says in *Holidays in Hell*, making fun of born-again Christians is like "hunting dairy cows with a high-powered rifle and scope." We all cringe when we read statements like this (even while we might be laughing), but we have to acknowledge they contain a kernel of truth. We do make ourselves ridiculous sometimes, publicly, privately and otherwise. We've all winced when we heard stories of Christian leaders who failed publicly. *Will that invalidate my faith in the eyes of my neighbors? Will it invalidate it in my own eyes?* When individual Christians do or say or promote stupid things, we all get the blame. And when we're honest, we can admit that sometimes it's we who are doing the stupid things.

THE CHURCH IS GLORIOUS

Both of us understand the messed-up-ness of the church. We both have had rough church experiences that are unusual. Or worse yet, maybe not so unusual. And yet we are both still here—because we not only understand the messed-up-ness of the church, but its glory.

JENN

I REMEMBER A TIME WHEN IT FELT ALMOST TOO PAINFUL to me to stay involved in church. Yet whenever I entertained thoughts of leaving, it seemed I'd hear someone's story about how the people in their church community were making a significant difference in their lives. I felt this sense of tension—on the one hand, all of this sin and messiness and sometimes downright unrepentance, but then on the other, these stories of redemption, hope and healing, which never erased the pain but somehow redeemed parts of it.

One of things that had the most significant impact on me was the confession of sexual sin by a pastor at my church. Although the details of the situation were not available to me, I was able to observe that the pastor was removed from his position but remained actively involved with the community and his wife and children. From my vantage point I could see that this church was committed to grace, community, healing and redemption. This was radically different from what I'd experienced in other churches with similar situations.

HEBREWS 10:24-25

And let us consider how we may spur one another on toward love and good deeds, not giving up meeting together, as some are in the habit of doing, but encouraging one another—and all the more as you see the Day approaching.

It was evident that they loved and believed in this leader and wanted to be involved in making a difference in his life. After some time passed, that pastor told the story of what had happened. He apologized to the entire church body and was gradually restored to an even more influential leadership role. He now leads from a much more powerful place of truth and authenticity.

That's the glory of the church: redemption. We worship a God "who gives life to the dead and calls into being things that were not" (Rom 4:17). And transforms them in the process. We, flawed and fallen, are the church. We, redeemed and transformed, are the church. The problem is in us, and the glory is in us. And it's all mixed up together. Yes, there's a stench inside the ark, but also an aroma of the knowledge of God (2 Cor 2:14).

There is something here that we whole-heartedly believe in and we want others to know and experience. We've experienced firsthand the tremendous redemption possible within the community of the church. We've seen people we love be forgiven, physically and emotionally healed, provided for financially, and embraced. They have received eternal life, held fast against addiction, resisted temptation, reconciled with estranged family members and found love. We are here because we want to be connected to these stories and to the remarkable, unexpected ways God reveals himself. We are here because we believe this is where we can find hope and truth and love. And God.

What does all this have to do with small groups?

We all hunger to be connected to something bigger than ourselves. Spirituality in the broadest sense can be defined as being connected to something bigger than ourselves or something beyond ourselves. In the ground-breaking book *Bowling Alone: The Collapse and Revival of American Community*, Robert Putnam explores the intrinsic desire for social bonds that reflect the desire to be part of something larger, as well as the detrimental effects that can result when we lack that connection. It seems we have an innate human desire to be known.

We believe that the church fulfills many intrinsic human needs, two of which are the need to be known and the need for connection to something bigger. The church connects people to the kingdom of God, and it simply doesn't get bigger than that. But relying on the local church congregations to fulfill all of our spiritual needs would be as ineffective as relying on the government to meet all of our financial needs. Resources are limited. Church staff members are usually overworked and underpaid. Some are white-knuckling their way, often feeling they lack permission to be real, to get too close to anyone, to operate in anything but "performance" mode. And still others are overwhelmed with expectations and caught up in mundane administrative tasks. Few churches have staff members who are paid to do nothing but address the spiritual needs of people.

As long as people desire to be connected to something bigger and to be known, they will be turning to churches—whatever form they may take—to fulfill those needs. And the best hope for the local church to move people toward an intimate relationship with the Lord is lay-led small groups—people gathering to wrestle with questions, beliefs, disappointment, disbelief, awe and so forth. Being in community makes us aware of the character of God in others and causes us to face what's going on inside ourselves. And sometimes groups help make us aware of those issues in ways that catalyze healing.

JENN

ONE SATURDAY AFTERNOON I CALLED THREE OF MY FRIENDS in my small group, including a woman who was my neighbor, to ask if anyone wanted to hang out that night. In each case, I got voicemail and left a message, but hadn't heard back from anyone as the evening approached. I was surprised to run into my neighbor in the driveway and hear that she was on her way to have dinner with all of the people I'd called that day. I was hurt and angry. I assumed that my voicemail messages were being ignored so that no one had to break the news to me that they were having dinner without me. In reality, no one had picked up my messages yet. They had all been engaged in working on a project together that day that kept them preoccupied. Even their attempts to fix the situation (repeated calls to include me) were met with a bit of suspicion. And then one friend realized they had to use more extreme measures. He showed up at my house unannounced and said, "You are coming to dinner with us."

Although my response was uncharacteristic of me in general, certain things were happening in my life at the time that contributed. Unless we're in community and letting people get close enough to disappoint us, we can sometimes fool ourselves into believing that things are better than they are. These friends—and this story along with many others—served as the catalyst I needed to move toward growth and restoration. They were close enough to me to trigger responses that I needed to look at more closely.

○   ○   ○

GROWTH AND COMMUNITY:
THE CHICKEN AND THE EGG

Small groups, a microcosm of the larger church, are designed to address those same two needs: to be known and to be connected to something bigger than ourselves. Yet many groups stop with the first and focus almost exclusively on relationships. Other groups major on the second and become intellectually based Bible studies, with people connecting to and learning the material but not being known themselves. The most effective small groups balance the Bible and life, and really, the two spheres were never designed to be separated.

One of the purposes of this book is to encourage groups to engage in Scripture in a relational way. Of all the resources we have in print, the Bible is by far the best for helping us know God. Yet it can be daunting to facilitators who have not studied it extensively or attended seminary. As a result, facilitators tend to rely almost exclusively on books that offer perspectives on and explanations of Scripture. Resources like these certainly can be helpful, but we also want facilitators to get more comfortable engaging with Scripture in small groups. And there are many ways to do that without needing to be an expert in exegesis and hermeneutics. Throughout this book we'll be mentioning ways to incorporate Scripture into groups. (Appendix one outlines additional thoughts on using Scripture in groups.)

While an academic, intellectual Bible study can be helpful for gaining knowledge, it forfeits a great deal of the power and life that relationships can bring, even the light they shed on the text. At the same time, groups that major on relationships with an occasional nod to Scripture also miss out on the power and purpose that the call to spiritual growth brings.

People want to know if there is something more—something bigger, something transcendent—and they want to connect to that. When we try to make groups all about *our* needs, *our* community, *our* relationships, they implode. We are unable to carry our own weight.

TARA

YEARS AGO I BELONGED TO A SMALL GROUP that was formed on a shared desire to grow and seek God. But as we met, the focus of the group became more about community and the individuals involved. Our conversations would often be about our jobs, relationship toils, and struggles. Good topics, but something crucial was overshadowed: our desire to know God.

Reflecting back on it now, I'm surprised at the amount of discussion that was self-focused, given the maturity and hearts of the people involved. One by one, members of the group started dropping out. But none of us could really explain why we were leaving, including me and Mark, my husband. Everyone in the group really liked each other—we were all friends outside the group.

It wasn't until after Mark and I left the group that we realized our deeper hunger for God had not been addressed there. Reflecting back on the experience, the self-focus was either not obvious or we were so self-focused we couldn't see the forest for the trees. The group eventually faded away. Sadly, I think we all shared that deeper hunger for God, yet we did not recognize that we were settling for less. Feelings were hurt along the way, and some friendships were damaged. How ironic that in our pursuit of community, community was lost.

A healthier direction is to make the primary goal of a group spiritual growth, and then create authentic community as the context for that larger purpose. Both are necessary, and prioritizing them in this way moves us toward a group experience that is more holistic, bringing the Bible and life back together in dynamic ways. Though spiritual growth can appear in different ways, and we'll say more on this later in the book, it is basically anything that moves us toward a deeper fullness of Christ. Although it's counterintuitive, if we aim first for growth, community will be stronger and healthier than if we aim first for community. Growth is the purpose—community is the context that makes growth effective.

When a group becomes self-focused, they are overlooking the deeper hunger for God, satisfying the flesh, not the soul. Such groups may work for a while before they eventually implode.

THE FRUIT OF HEALTHY SMALL GROUPS

We've seen and experienced the difference small groups make. We know firsthand the spiritual growth and transformation that can happen in authentic community. Although it's hard to measure the effectiveness of small groups because the "results" are so anecdotal, the real results lie in the stories that emerge. And those stories are all different.

One woman was sent to our city by her husband after having an affair. Here in a city where she only knew her parents and two old friends, she took steps to get connected—through those friends—with a small group at our church. She shared openly, developed friendships, worshiped and connected with others in spiritual fellowship and learning. Through that group she became connected with a support group, which in time she went on to lead. She experienced a great deal of healing during her time here. The marriage survived and she and her husband are committed to the uphill battle they face. The friends who connected her to the group had very little to do with the healing that took place in her life; it was the strangers she met along the way—the brothers and sisters in Christ who embraced her and extended grace—who really made a difference.

That kind of spiritual nurturing and growth happens best when people are actively cultivating their relationship with God. Without that focus on our life with God, we are likely to judge rather than extend grace or put up barriers rather than reach out. The intentional cultivation of our life with God is the example set for us by the first Christians. "They devoted themselves to the apostles' teaching and to fellowship, to the breaking of bread and to prayer" (Acts 2:42). People will know God better if they are in a community where they are known, have a place to bring their questions and have people alongside them on the journey of growth—a place where people are unafraid to say the hard things, but say them out of love.

One friend, Charlene, entered into a hospital chaplaincy program. She believed comfort in times of crisis was important work and wanted to become competent in the area. After several weeks of concerted effort in this area, her supervisor took her aside and said, "I know how much you want to be able to do this kind of work. And I believe that with practice you can do it. However, you might want to consider that this may not be your primary area of giftedness. In fact, I've observed the way you naturally seem to lead the team and plan the time, and I would encourage you to consider developing your gifts in leadership, administration and strategic thinking. Those can be used by God just as much."

THE RIVER

These are not new thoughts, but rather the perspectives we are holding as we write this book. There are already many books written that tout the role and importance of small groups. We want to give you some ideas and skills to use to increase the effect your small group has on the spiritual growth of others. New ways of doing old things. Again, this is not a program but rather a way to equip people with valuable and timeless skills regardless of the purpose or format of the group.

A small group is like a river. And the goal of a facilitator is to find the natural flow of that river and move along with it. The facilitator doesn't control the group or push it forward. As a river moves along, it takes on a life of its own, gaining its own momentum and drawing from its own natural energy.

A river has a starting point, a water source, from which it begins to flow. The facilitator often has the most influence at this point, as the group draws from the initial leading of the Holy Spirit, who inspires its beginning. But generally the facilitator is unable to see too far along the river's course, or make it go where he or she wants. The Spirit may have different ideas. Although the banks the facilitator creates through the discussion provide guidance for the direction of the river, they don't ultimately control it, for the river is running of its own accord. Sometimes the terrain changes and the course shifts.

During some stretches the river rushes along, picking up speed, while at other times it just seems to trickle, making hardly any visible progress at all. There can be still places and undertows that don't look dangerous but are. Sometimes the river hits rocky patches or even rushes over a waterfall. Then it rains and the water overruns the banks, creating streams that branch off from the original course of the river. Eventually, rivers come to a delta, where the waters run into the ocean. Or they gradually slow their flow, allowing their water to be absorbed into dry ground. Then the cycle starts over again, with evaporation, clouds, rainfall and snow in the mountains.

The title *Finding the Flow* references this metaphor of a river, while also paying homage to Mihaly Csikszentmihalyi's book *Flow*, which talks about optimal experience—that execptionally rewarding feeling of being "in the zone" when you are doing well something that you enjoy. That's not a place we live most of the time, but as group failitators or participants you've probably experienced moments of that, where the group just seems to flow.

Our hope is that this book will help provide you with the skills that allow that experience of flow to happen more frequently—and in ways that result in others being drawn toward Christ in authentic ways. Perhaps we'll make a difference in someone's life. Perhaps. Maybe an addiction will be overcome, an affair will be prevented, or someone will feel accepted or loved or secure. But along the way there will also be disappointments and failures. These are part of the course of the river as well. We're dealing with people, and we're all unfinished projects. We can only lead or influence others as far as we have gone ourselves, so the focus needs to be on who we are as people and what we can do with the gifts God has given us.

So in as nonprogrammatic a way as possible, we offer a fresh look at skills for group facilitators that will hopefully result in people being transformed through knowing God better. Again, new ways of doing old things. Very old things.

1

THE WATER SOURCE

Knowing Yourself

> *Those who listen to the word but*
> *do not do what it says are like*
> *people who look at their faces*
> *in a mirror and, after looking*
> *at themselves, go away and*
> *immediately forget what they*
> *look like.*
>
> *But those who look intently into*
> *the perfect law that gives freedom*
> *and continue in it— not forgetting*
> *what they have heard, but doing*
> *it—they will be blessed in*
> *what they do.*
>
> JAMES 1:23-25

Some small group facilitators seem to have an instinct for it. They start a group and it just takes off—even if they haven't led one before. Why? Is it giftedness? Personality? Skills? All of those certainly play a part, as does the mystery of why the Holy Spirit chooses to bless some things and not others.

TARA

PART OF MY ROLE AS A SMALL GROUPS PASTOR was to visit the groups once in a while, encourage the leaders, see how things were going, do a heresy check and so forth. The following are a few experiences I had in visiting a few start-up groups. As you read about each group, guess which ones were thriving a year later, and why.

Group 1. I walked into one living room and was greeted by a high buzz of energy. I overheard several snatches of conversation as people were coming in. "So you started the new job? That's great! I'm so glad I was able to connect you with Rob on that. Sounds like a great fit all around." "Did you go to the rescue mission last week? I really wanted to join you guys, but I had family in town. Are you going again next month?" "This is Emily. I work with her at the hospital and invited her to join us tonight." So much was going on, it would have been hard to get a word in edgewise. When we sat down, there were announcements about the snack schedule, who would be facilitating the discussions in upcoming weeks (all regulars were expected to take turns), what group service projects were coming up, and a request that we begin praying even now about who might want to lead a branch of the group at another location, as Heather's small living room wasn't going to be able to hold the group forever. By the time they got around to the actual study, the group time was more than half over. These facilitators made their group about service and outreach.

Group 2. A few nights later I walked into a second living room, a much quieter room this time. Everyone in this group had remembered their Bibles, so no one had to crane their necks and look over others' shoulders. The facilitator opened the time with a ten-minute presentation on what he'd discovered in researching this section of the Sermon on the Mount. Everyone listened attentively. When the discussion started, it started in earnest. People talked excitedly about the meaning of the passage, the cultural context and how Jesus would have meant for us to apply it today. During the prayer-request time at the end, they shared what was going on in their lives and asked for accountability and support in living godly lives. This facilitator made his group about knowing and living out the Scriptures.

Group 3. The next week I entered a third living room, where five people gathered to read and discuss a book. They made up the core of the new group, and had all arrived a bit early. Due in part to their personalities, the group was welcoming as others arrived. Great snacks were on the counter, and laughter and music filled the background. A few people relatively new to the group arrived and were greeted "Norm style" as they walked in the front door. People seemed to feel accepted no matter where they were spiritually. Growth, challenging each other and prayer were almost afterthoughts. At the end of the night, everyone was invited to Carol's birthday party on Monday night and to help Pete move on Saturday. These facilitators made their group about inclusivity and assimilation.

A year later, they were all thriving.

Every time I visited groups, whether they were just getting off the ground or had been around for years, the one thing that stood out every time was how different they all were from each other. They all had distinct personalities and "vibes." Even when the material was the same, the groups felt different. And it wasn't a better-worse thing—just different. The facilitators, and consequently the groups, had different spiritual-gift mixes and different personalities.

Much has been written about spiritual gifts and which ones are most helpful for facilitating small groups. There isn't always agreement about that, though. Some would emphasize the warmth and safety that hospitality and encouragement can bring (group 3). Others would stress the importance of teaching and exhortation for spiritual growth (group 2). Still others would suggest leadership and discernment, with an eye toward multiplication of groups (group 1). The truth is, successful group facilitators can come in any of these combinations, plus many others.

And personality certainly has a role in facilitation. Maybe we need to find extroverted charismatic types to lead groups—they certainly can draw a crowd. But then introverted contemplative people make such good listeners and shepherds. And there's a lot to be said for entrepreneurial business people or intellectual teachers as well. As with spiritual gifts, there's no "right answer" here. All spiritual gifts are good for serving others. Groups are so versatile that they call for many different areas of personality and giftedness—and many different combinations can work equally well.

DO THIS

With which of these three groups did you experience the most resonance? How about dissonance? It can be eye-opening to know what's important to you in small group experiences—and what's not.

So, if we can't pinpoint facilitation success to a particular gifting or personality, perhaps we should focus on skill acquisition. Indeed, most small group leader training focuses on skills: listening, asking questions, facilitating, developing others, resolving conflict. (And if you've looked at our table of contents, you'll see that we agree that these areas are important.) Generally, leader trainings give a nod to the leader having a consistent personal devotion time or living a godly example for others, but then they quickly move on to skills.

But skill acquisition isn't the place to start either. Those who want to be better leaders need to start by developing their self-awareness, and they need to take it beyond spiritual gifts. Most, if not all, gifts are helpful for facilitating a small group. And virtually all leadership skills can be taught, but do you know which come most naturally to you? Spiritual disciplines certainly play an important role too, but which are most important for each of us to practice regularly—and in which ways—given our individual personalities and the seasons of our spiritual journeys? That may look different for many of us. What really makes a difference is when facilitators know what lies in their heart, what's really important to them, how they tend to respond and why. It makes a difference when they know that their unique facilitation style will come from that authentic, personal place. And it makes a difference that they seek God for growth and direction along the way. When facilitators practice self-awareness, they are many times more likely to see the work of God in others, and to recognize it when God is working in—and on—themselves.

Now, some would say that self-awareness puts the focus in the wrong place—"It's not about me. It's all about God." True, God outranks us in the "deserving of focus" category. Yet he makes it clear through Scripture that he is paying attention to us—both to our hearts and to our actions. After all, only a fool looks in the mirror and then walks away forgetting what he or she has seen.

This chapter acknowledges that a small group experience starts with the facilitator. That's why it's so important for the facilitator to know who he or she is as a person. The facilitator, with the guidance of the Holy Spirit, creates the water source that the rest of the river flows from.

Jehoshaphat, a somewhat obscure Old Testament character, serves as an illustration (2 Chronicles 20:1-30). In the beginning of the story Jehoshaphat, king of Judah, is informed that vast armies are approaching Judah to take over its territory. His response to this news tells us a lot about his character, including his spiritual gifts, disciplines and values.

By reading his story we could assume that one of Jehoshaphat's main spiritual gifts is faith. His immediate response to the threat of a battle is to seek the Lord and ask the nation to fast.

> Alarmed, Jehoshaphat resolved to inquire of the LORD, and he proclaimed a fast for all Judah. (v. 3)

He expresses his faith in God as he prays before the masses of people who have assembled:

> Then Jehoshaphat stood up in the assembly of Judah and Jerusalem at the temple of the LORD in the front of the new courtyard and said:

"LORD, the God of our ancestors, are you not the God who is in heaven? You rule over all the kingdoms of the nations. Power and might are in your hand, and no one can withstand you.

"Our God, will you not judge them? For we have no power to face this vast army that is attacking us. We do not know what to do, but our eyes are on you." (vv. 5-6, 12)

The magnitude of his faith is further expressed by his willingness to trust and obey the words of a prophet:

He said: "Listen, King Jehoshaphat and all who live in Judah and Jerusalem! This is what the LORD says to you: 'Do not be afraid or discouraged because of this vast army. For the battle is not yours, but God's. Tomorrow march down against them. They will be climbing up by the Pass of Ziz, and you will find them at the end of the gorge in the Desert of Jeruel. You will not have to fight this battle. Take up your positions; stand firm and see the deliverance the LORD will give you, Judah and Jerusalem. Do not be afraid; do not be discouraged. Go out to face them tomorrow, and the LORD will be with you.'" (vv. 15-17)

And Jehoshaphat's faith is again emphasized by how he rallies the troops before going to face the armies:

Early in the morning they left for the Desert of Tekoa. As they set out, Jehoshaphat stood and said, "Listen to me, Judah and people of Jerusalem! Have faith in the LORD your God and you will be upheld; have faith in his prophets and you will be successful." (v. 20)

We also know from these verses that his spiritual disciplines include prayer and fasting. Giftedness and spiritual disciplines are undoubtedly important in facilitating small groups, and we encourage people to pursue knowledge of them. But much has been written about them already, so we don't want to spend our time here repeating things people have already heard many times.

Instead, we want to focus on the other things revealed about Jehoshaphat that also contributed to his success. We will start by focusing on two areas that give great insight into how each person is wired: values and emotional intelligence. Both knowing our values and developing emotional intelligence create paths to knowing ourselves and developing self-awareness.

VALUES

Values is one of those loaded words we mentioned in the introduction. What comes to mind when you hear the word *values?* Family values, the value wars, good Christian values, right versus wrong? Let's make this really clear at the outset: that is *not* what we mean here. The way we are using *values* is not "these are the right answers and those are the wrong answers." One facilitator may value staying on track and ending on time, while another may value letting the time unfold more organically and adapting the group time to the needs of the evening. There is a place for both.

Values are an expression of your inner workings, essentially understanding what's really important to you as a small group facilitator. And that starts with knowing what's important to you personally, for the two are always related. Your values are the filter you pass all of your experiences through to determine if they are satisfactory or not. Your own experiences, your relationship with Jesus, your culture—all of these play a part in your unique value system. Values express the desires of your heart, and they come out in everything you do: parenting, the work you choose and the way you lead your group. But they also may come out in very practical ways, like whether you tend to stay on track during your small group gatherings. To better know yourself, it's helpful to describe your values and why certain experiences are positive or negative for you.

Going back to the story of Jehoshaphat, what can we assume some of his values were? What seems to be revealed about his heart and his priorities? How does this affect his leadership? Another look at the Scripture reveals that he values:

- *Obedience to God.* He both seeks the Lord's direction and follows the advice of a prophet (vv. 3, 15).

- *Justice.* He reminds God that he did not allow his people to take over the territory of the nations that were about to attack Judah when they could have done so successfully. Therefore, it would be unfair for those nations to now be victorious against God's people:

> But now here are men from Ammon, Moab and Mount Seir, whose territory you would not allow Israel to invade when they came from Egypt; so they turned away from them and did not destroy them. See how they are repaying us by coming to drive us out of the possession you gave us as an inheritance. (vv. 10-11)

- *Worship.* In this story, corporate worship of God comes just as they are going into battle:

> Jehoshaphat bowed down with his face to the ground, and all the people of Judah and Jerusalem fell down in worship before the LORD. . . .
>
> After consulting the people, Jehoshaphat appointed men to sing to the LORD and to praise him for the splendor of his holiness as they went out at the head of the army, saying:
> "Give thanks to the LORD,
>   for his love endures forever." (vv. 18, 21)

- *Celebration.* He leads the celebration of the victory over the enemies:

> Then, led by Jehoshaphat, all the men of Judah and Jerusalem returned joyfully to Jerusalem, for the LORD had given them cause to rejoice over their enemies. They entered Jerusalem and went to the temple of the LORD with harps and lyres and trumpets. (vv. 27-28)

We can't be sure of Jehoshaphat's values, but his choices and responses tell a story about who he is as a person. They reveal something about his heart, and they affect his leadership.

UNDERSTANDING YOUR VALUES

Scripture is a great place to go to understand your own values. The stories that you are most drawn to are likely an expression of your values. Are you drawn to the story of Joseph? Perhaps you value patience, hard work, gaining favor, redemption and reconciliation. If it's the story of Moses, you might value open conversation with God, partnership with others or leadership. Or how about Esther? Your values may include being chosen, doing the right thing or God's orchestration of events and circumstances. A new way to look at Scripture is to get curious about what resonates with you and how that reveals what you value.

Another way to understand what you value is to reflect on times in your own life when you really felt like you were in the flow, on top of your game or in your element.

DO THIS

What is your favorite story from the Bible? What does that story reveal about what is important to you? See appendix two for a list of possible personal values, and circle the ones that are present in the story.

TARA

A FEW YEARS AGO I WAS TAKING A COACH TRAINING seminar taught by Jenn. We didn't know each other very well at the time. Jenn asked for a volunteer for an exercise, and I stepped forward. The only instruction given was to share a peak experience. This could be from any area of life: work, family, ministry, anything. After thinking for a moment, I shared about the first time I taught a college class as an adjunct instructor. Here's what I said:

"I was in graduate school and was only twenty-four, and we were given the opportunity to be T.A.s—teaching assistants. In the English department this meant I would be given a freshman writing class for the semester. So "teaching assistant" was really kind of a misnomer—I wasn't assisting anyone, and I would be the only "professor" the students would see. I was pretty nervous about it and didn't feel qualified. I mean, shouldn't they be more careful to have people in there who knew what they were doing? But they trusted me and that felt good. It was such a great opportunity, I couldn't pass it up, so I decided to go ahead with it. I selected a textbook, created a syllabus, planned the lessons, everything on my own. The first day of class I was so nervous I thought I was going to pass out. I thought, they'll take one look at me and know I don't belong here and that I shouldn't be doing this. But they didn't. Over the course of the semester, the class went great—the students engaged in discussion, worked on their writing skills, seemed to be learning. I couldn't believe it—it was working, and working well! I was doing the grading and the lesson planning, coming up with my own ideas on how to get things across. It was so exciting to be able to do that on my own at only twenty-four and feel like it was going well. I had a great relationship with the students. Although I went on to teach more classes in the future, that was one of my favorites. And at the end of the semester, my student evaluations came back really positive."

DO THIS

Journal about a few of the peak experiences you've had in your lifetime, times when you have felt you were in the flow. Include your best and worst experiences as a small group facilitator. Then ask yourself, *What do these experiences say about what I think is important?* As you consider your own values, think about how they might apply to your facilitation of a small group. What qualities do you prefer in a group experience? What would you be enthusiastic about? How might a small groups pastor most effectively come alongside and support you?

After telling about that peak experience, Jenn said to me, "Okay, based on what you've told me, I'm going to reflect back some of what I've heard you say. You appreciated that your abilities were recognized, that they believed in you even though you didn't have the credentials of a professor. You like to be able to create your own structures and material, you feel respected when you are given a good deal of freedom and responsibility. You seem to have a respect for established authority structures, sometimes lack internal confidence but are willing to risk anyway. I hear that in your work you value credentials, recognition, trust, autonomy, competence and respect. I imagine you probably really dislike being micromanaged." I was stunned. Although Jenn didn't really know me at the time, she had absolutely nailed so many of the things I consider important in life—not just in teaching, but in life. What she said could easily have been generalized to just about any area of my life.

○   ○   ○

Whether we're talking about Jehoshaphat leading a nation or Tara leading a classroom of students, anyone who understands his or her values and makes choices to honor those values has a much better opportunity to be deeply satisfied. And deep satisfaction results in energy and enthusiasm that draws people in—ideally into a place where the image of God is noticed in that person.

VALUES PLAYING OUT IN SMALL GROUPS

MY HUSBAND, MARK, AND I CO-LED A SMALL GROUP about a year after we got married. After the group time ended and everyone went home, we'd usually sit out on our apartment balcony and debrief. For several weeks in a row, Mark thought things were going great, but I was feeling impatient, like the group wasn't going anywhere. I'd been prepping the material, but things kept getting off track. People were talking a lot and sharing things that were going on in their lives, but it didn't seem to me like the comments were rooted in much of anything or had much direction. But then one night, I felt like things finally took off—I had a sense that we were finally getting somewhere! Sitting outside on the balcony afterward, I told Mark that it seemed like this time people really engaged with the material and got interested in discussing the passage, and the ideas really started flying. Mark thought for a minute and responded, "It was okay, I guess. It just didn't seem very relationally connected tonight."

For those of you who recognize a familiar dynamic here, I'll give you some supporting evidence. Mark is a therapist, and at that time I was a teacher. He's more of a feeler, and I'm more of a thinker. Although both of us value relational connection *and* engaging with ideas around a passage of Scripture, we don't value those in exactly equal amounts.

○   ○   ○

If you are passing your facilitation experience through a filter (that is, your values) and concluding it was either favorable or unfavorable without knowing what filter you are passing it through, you will likely become confused, getting stuck in your head trying to figure it out. And that may interfere with what the Spirit of God is trying to accomplish. On the other hand, if you know your values, you can concentrate more on what would have made the experience more favorable, assess what would have been most helpful for others in the group, and decide which values to strengthen next time.

DO THIS

Facilitating a small group that aligns closely with your values will reduce the likelihood of burnout or boredom. Incorporate something simple every week that honors one of your values. Example: If having fun is a value of yours, include funny movie clips, quotes, cartoons or songs that illustrate what you'll be discussing.

One of the biggest blind spots with values is that we can tend to think our own values are the most important. Like in Tara's previous example, one facilitator might say, "You obviously don't care about Scripture." And the other facilitator could respond, "You obviously don't care about people." Clearly, both would have missed the boat because both elements are absolutely essential in every healthy small group.

It's kind of like spiritual gifts: they're all needed to make things work well. It's easy to value your own gifts to the exclusion of others: "It's really all about evangelism; the rest is window dressing." We sometimes feel that everyone should share our highest values as their primary focus. Thus we can't understand, for example, why someone else might talk so much about how art is the purest form of worship, and how excellence in music and painting and the creation of sacred space brings glory to God. When we focus on our own gifts and passions to the exclusion of others, we can both end up imbalanced and feeling like we're speaking different languages. Often this results in increased polarization.

Or on the other hand, sometimes we wish we had a different gift mix. Someone recently observed that a friend of ours has the gift of prophecy, and that friend responded with an utter lack of enthusiasm, "Yes, I know. I'm so tired of having that gift. No one ever listens to prophets, and they certainly don't like them." Often we look around at our culture, even our church's culture, to see what gifts are valued and then consequently minimize the significance and necessity of our own gifts.

The same is true with values. We think some are better than others, that some are more holy or more godly. We add our shoulds and should nots.

A friend of ours shared with us that it's taken him time to accept that one of his values is liking nice things. He's tried to make sense of why he has this value. Is it because he was raised without the means for having nice things? Or because he's learned over time that you get what you pay for? And after becoming a follower of Christ, he spent several years feeling guilty about this value, especially after making an expensive purchase. After all, he *should* be more modest and generous to others, shouldn't he? He *should* give his money to people who are in need.

He tried to disown this value, judging it as lacking virtue. But it seemed the more he disowned it, the more power it had over him, the more guilt he felt, and the more he judged people who had nice houses, cars and the latest gadgets.

In a similar way, a group leader could say, "I shouldn't value large numbers turning out for my group—I shouldn't put so much emphasis on that. Remember what happened when David took the census? I'm supposed to put my trust in God, not numbers." In a different church, numbers might be highly valued, and someone could say, "I kind of like investing in just a few people, but I know I should be reaching out and trying to include more. I need to have something more tangible to show for my efforts—like a really large group."

A more helpful approach, both personally and as a small group facilitator, is to be honest about what you want. From that place of honesty, you can decide how to honor God. Our friend came to accept that liking nice things is okay, that there really isn't anything inherently sinful about it. He also realized it can even be environmentally responsible. Although high quality items are more expensive, he realized he consumes less in the long run. Over time he has become more willing to accept this value. With acceptance comes freedom. Paradoxically, it wasn't freedom to consume and purchase more nice things. It was the freedom of choice. The freedom from the *shoulds*. And what he found was that he started *wanting* to be more responsible as a consumer. He also *wanted* to give more to people in need. This shift in how he viewed his values freed him to consider and honor other values and responsibilities he felt he had as a follower of Jesus.

Once we know what our values are, we need to find ways to live them out in our groups and in the rest of our lives. In that way, our lives become a more accurate reflection of who we really are. For example, what

MORE ON VALUES

Our values are uniquely our own. We are each uniquely designed to glorify God in a way that only we can. When we honor our values, we find that we have more enthusiasm and energy, the oomph required to press onward.

Understanding our own values might also help us understand the motives of our heart and the areas where our will might be incongruent with God's.

The values of people in the group may compete with each other (holding to the stated agenda versus willingness to shift direction, efficient use of time versus powerful moments, or structure versus following the Holy Spirit).

are some of the ways our friend lives out his value of liking nice things? He bought a nice house, but a small one that is environmentally responsible (energy efficient, built with recycled materials). He also owns a nice car, but shares it with his wife so they can be a one-car family, walking and using public transportation, not having a car payment.

Identifying our values—without immediately judging them—can help us in various ways:

- giving us the freedom to be authentic in serving God and others
- broadening the values that are honored in our groups rather than getting fixated on the "shoulds"
- seeing our values as responsibilities to God and others rather than as excuses to justify our decisions
- being more intentional in facilitating a group and creating direction
- understanding why we feel the way we do when the group shifts or changes direction
- compensating for our values if we discern that they aren't really what the rest of the group needs most right now, or where God is leading the group
- realizing that others have different values, and that's not a bad thing
- balancing with other people's values and drawing on the strengths of cofacilitators

DO THIS

Help the people in your small group identify their values by asking them all to share with the group a peak experience from their life. Ask the group to describe what seems important to each person sharing. (See appendix two for a list of personal values.)

Values include things like holding to the stated agenda, spontaneity, advance planning, powerful moments, vulnerability, sense of humor, intellectual depth and so on. For a more thorough (although far from comprehensive) listing of small group values, see the values exercise in appendix three. Values vary widely between individuals, and will affect the nature of the group being led. Although any combination of values can coexist, note that at times, certain values can compete with each other (e.g., holding to the stated agenda versus a willingness to shift direction, efficient use of time versus powerful moments).

I KNOW . . . SO NOW WHAT?

Once we've identified our values, we can decide what to do with them. This kind of self-awareness allows us to check in with ourselves. If you feel like your group is falling apart, check that it's not an issue of conflicting values. To a large degree, your values determine how you feel about group members attending a baseball game together instead of doing the study, or group members focusing on raising up more leaders and branching out rather than building deeper relationships. Sometimes what's best for the group doesn't align with your own values, and a self-aware facilitator can recognize those times. And hopefully he or she will be humble enough to accept that group life is not always about what's personally most pleasing.

TARA

SELF-AWARENESS ALSO ALLOWS US TO COMPENSATE by empowering others with different values. Once I was working with a woman named Alyssa who wanted to start a group. She had a great deal of vision and drive (she's now working in humanitarian missions overseas), and I asked her what kind of coleader might be most helpful for her. After thinking for a minute, Alyssa said, "Someone who can remember names. I tend to focus on the vision and direction, and forget about the niceties. I need someone who greets people when they arrive, asks them about themselves, follows up about things they shared last week that were going on in their lives. And you know, now that I'm thinking of it, I know just the person!" Alyssa's new coleader was a bubbly extrovert who loved to host, asked people questions and, yes, even remembered their names.

○   ○   ○

Sometimes we will even discover competing values within ourselves: what happens when one value is being in the moment and following whatever comes up in a discussion, and another value is beginning and ending on time? It's a struggle and takes prayer and a conscious decision, at times sacrificing one for the other.

And if something you believe is a value comes up that truly isn't honoring to God, there's nothing like good old-fashioned repentance and confession. Values are inherently good, but as it is with many of our qualities and characteristics, there is the potential for a dark side. It's possible to discover that what you really want from a group is to gain some kind of glory, draw attention to yourself, have an adoring audience or create a platform to discuss your pet ideas. The church won't let you preach to the whole congregation, so you might as well lead a group. If issues like these come up, recognize and confess them, and talk about them with a coleader or other trusted person. We don't need to have perfect motives to facilitate a group, but we do need to acknowledge what's going on and keep impure motives in check. And that frees us up to lead from our real strengths.

DO THIS

Complete the values clarification exercise in appendix three along with your coleader, then compare results. The ways your values are similar or different can be a helpful way to make sure your values are aligned or complementary.

God will use us in a different way than he might use someone else. And that's good. So (1) be aware of who you are, and (2) don't try to be someone else. Don't try to imitate some really good facilitator who appears to be making a difference. Don't be too persuaded by the person who held the position before you. Don't try to apply a formula. When we are facilitating in a way that honors our values, the same thing happens as when we are using our gifts. We experience flow, lose track of time and enjoy the experience—it's natural and satisfying. Magical things happen and God is glorified.

EMOTIONAL INTELLIGENCE

Knowing ourselves and our values contributes to what we call emotional intelligence. Emotional intelligence is a theory popularized in *Emotional Intelligence* by Daniel Goleman, and it involves understanding our feelings (and those of others) for the sake of learning how to express them rather than letting them interfere with our relationships, motivation or what we're trying to accomplish. Goleman's research revealed that emotional intelligence is even more important to a person's success in work and life than intelligence.

Let's refer back to Jehoshaphat. We are told that he consults the people.

> After consulting the people, Jehoshaphat appointed men to sing to the LORD and to praise him for the splendor of his holiness. (2 Chronicles 20:21)

Does this seem strange? He's the king, after all. It doesn't say he consulted his generals but rather the people. And he follows their advice to march into the battle singing and praising God. So what's going on there? Was he trying to influence others by involving them in the decision—to ensure he would get their support? Was he showing his commitment to team work? Did he feel empathy toward a people whose promises from God were being threatened? Or did he know himself well enough to know that he lacked wisdom in this area and that counsel was critical? (From what we learn later in the chapter about his partnership with an evil man [2 Chronicles 20:35] we can be pretty certain that he lacked at least some wisdom.) If we could answer yes to one or all of these questions, it would point to his emotional intelligence.

At the very least, we know that Jehoshaphat stayed calm in the face of great threat and distress. He maintained his

DO THIS

Once you've established your top five values as a small group facilitator (appendix three), set goals for your group around each of these values. For example, if you value large numbers, establish the number of people you want to attend your small group by a certain date. Determine what you could do to motivate others in your group to help you reach your goal.

composure and his ability to think clearly. His emotions or fears did not hijack reason, and he did not act on impulse. He helped manage others' emotions by praying and entreating God to intervene. He listened to others, maintained motivation and motivated others. He gave people assignments according to their strengths. He inspired others. He never lost hope for the future of Judah or stopped trust-

Table 1.1. Emotional Intelligence

Emotional Intelligence Summarized	
(Adapted from Primal Leadership: Learning to Lead with Emotional Intelligence by *Daniel Goleman, Richard Boyatzis and Annie McKee [Boston: Harvard Business School Press, 2002].)*	
Personal Competence (and associated behaviors)	**Social Competence** (and associated behaviors)
Self-awareness—the ability to read one's emotions and recognize their impact while trusting gut instincts to guide decisions. ▪ Being able to name one's emotion when it's occurring ▪ Accurate assessment of strengths and weaknesses ▪ Self-confidence ▪ Trusting "gut instinct"	**Social awareness** (understanding others)—the ability to sense, understand and react to others' emotions while comprehending relationships that exist between people and groups. ▪ Being able to name another's emotion when it's occurring ▪ Responding appropriately to those emotions ▪ Empathizing with others ▪ Recognizing and meeting others' needs
Self-management—involves controlling one's emotions and impulses and adapting to changing circumstances. ▪ Motivating oneself and persisting in the face of frustrations; remaining optimistic ▪ Delaying gratification ▪ Keeping distress from swamping the ability to think clearly ▪ Making decisions consistent with personal values ▪ Adaptability and initiative	**Relationship management** (leading and working with others)—the ability to inspire, influence, and develop others while managing conflict. ▪ Identifying others' strengths and developing them ▪ Setting an example that inspires others ▪ Taking appropriate steps to address conflict ▪ Leading change ▪ Influencing others

ing in the God he served. He exhibited great emotional intelligence. *Emotional intelligence* may be a relatively new phrase rooted in current research, but as concepts go, it's a really old one.

PERSONAL COMPETENCIES IN SMALL GROUPS

The personal competencies outlined in the left column of table 1.1 are especially helpful in small group settings because when passions surge—as they often do given the topics discussed in small groups— the emotional mind has the ability to hijack the logical mind, which may have negative consequences. As small group leaders, it's important to know ourselves—our triggers, biases and tendencies—so we don't allow them to interfere with the group experience. Sometimes our emotions may cause us to respond inappropriately, damaging the group dynamic. Understanding our particular triggers and identifying them in the moment can help prevent our emotions from gaining the upper hand over what we're trying to accomplish. But often much of the emotional life is unconscious. Awareness— the bringing into consciousness—allows us to make choices, such as shaking off a bad mood or responding well to another's behavior.

DO THIS

When something said in the small group triggers you in a negative way, ask the group to respond to the comment. This approach will buy you time to determine what, if anything, to do about your emotion. From there you can decide how you want to contribute to the conversation.

A woman named Jamie was facilitating a small group, and Ben, who always sat directly across from her, seemed to be constantly fidgeting and making clicking noises. Ben was looking around everywhere except at whoever was talking. Jamie found herself getting increasingly irritated by Ben's behavior and realized she was not making the effort that she usually would to include him in the discussion. She found herself hoping that he would drop out if he was so bored by what they were talking about. Finally, one night after the meeting Jamie was talking with another group member who mentioned that Ben was struggling with severe ADD (attention deficit disorder) and was trying to focus on the content they were discussing because he really wanted to learn. Jamie's interpretation of the situation did a 180, and she later said that had she been more self-aware of her propensity to take things personally (e.g., he must be bored because I'm not doing a good job) she would have handled the situation much differently, going to greater lengths to recognize and correctly interpret the situation.

By the way, often the same triggers we have in our close relationships or at work are those that will appear in our groups. Jamie realized through this experience that she was dealing with the same issue at work: she often feared that she was not performing well enough on the job, so she would look for indirect signs of approval or disapproval rather than asking directly for feedback. So if you're stumped when thinking in the context of small groups, think in the context of work or family or friendship. You'll likely see some running themes.

DO THIS

Improving your ability to notice and name emotions will lead to developing greater emotional intelligence. After each small group gathering, take five minutes to write down all of the emotions you noticed during the meeting—both your own and others'. If you have trouble naming the emotion, try using the list of emotions in appendix four.

Many times when we run into a problem facilitating a group, the problem is not rooted in skill areas but in our emotions (or a lack of understanding of our emotions) that prevents us from effectively reaching our goals. Whether it's a lack of self-confidence that prevents us from taking risks or a drive to prove our worth that comes across looking like arrogance, we all have something that gets in our way. Awareness of those areas can be painful, but it's a necessary first step in overcoming the issues that block us.

SOCIAL COMPETENCIES IN SMALL GROUPS

Let's go back to table 1.1 on emotional intelligence. It's important to note that personal competencies (the left column), with an emphasis on self-awareness, are the bedrock of emotional intelligence. The more we know ourselves, the more skilled we will be in the social competence (right column) areas.

For instance, after we gain awareness of our own emotions, we'll be more adept at intuiting another's feelings (empathizing). In small groups we often do this by reading nonverbal clues. If one person in the group is a bit brusque, a facilitator may read nonverbal cues to notice that another group member may have felt hurt by that behavior. A change in posture, unwillingness to make eye contact or a furrowed brow may be the only indication we have of someone's feelings. Being able to notice those cues and determine when it's appropriate to inquire about them will lead to some of the most powerful dialogue in small groups.

DO THIS

When in your group you believe you've experienced and identified someone's emotion, name it and inquire about it. Asking will allow the person the opportunity to clarify or expand on that emotion. Or not. It's important to give them a choice. Understanding his or her emotion will help you and the group develop empathy for each other.

Unfortunately, one of the best ways to learn to identify emotions in people and determine whether to ask about them is simply trial and error. Facilitators can begin by taking people aside after the group time ends to discuss how a comment or discussion affected them. Eventually, facilitators can move on to making those inquiries during the small group meeting itself so the group becomes more comfortable engaging with each others' emotions. Opening the process up to the group provides opportunities for others to strengthen their emotional intelligence as well.

In the area of relationship management (see table 1.1) the topics are so critical that two other chapters will be devoted to them: dealing with conflict and developing other leaders.

INCREASING YOUR EMOTIONAL INTELLIGENCE QUOTIENT

Just as we can learn a lot about ourselves by knowing our values, it's also helpful to understand some of the things we do as facilitators that get in the way of developing our own emotional intelligence or forming an emotionally intelligent small group (table 1.2). Increasing our emotional intelligence includes knowing the group, its boundaries and when it's time to take to take it deeper.

Scripture is one the best places to go for examples of emotional intelligence, or lack thereof. Many biblical stories provide stunning examples of low emotional intelligence. In the first fifty pages alone, we can find story after story. Cain kills his brother Abel because he can't manage his emotions of jealousy and anger. Later Sarai, unable to delay gratification, asks her husband, Abram, to conceive a child with her maid rather that waiting for the Lord to fulfill his promise of many descendents. Then

Table 1.2. Common Mistakes Facilitators Make That Get in the Way of Forming Emotionally Intelligent Small Groups

Unwilling to be uncomfortable or go to difficult and emotional places
Pressuring oneself to have it all together (prevents authenticity and vulnerability)
Not bouncing back after a negative experience
Taking too much control (e.g., putting people on the spot, enforcing a rigid agenda, having to have the right answer, not sharing responsibility)
Not experientially understanding the topics being discussed, keeping the conversation theoretical
Undealt-with business around discussion topics
Neglecting to fill in one's weak spots in leadership with others' strengths
Resisting change or holding too tightly to the original direction for the group
Overlooking conflict among group members with the hope it will work itself out
Not setting a positive example as a leader
Taking complaints about the group too personally; letting frustrations interfere with progress
Being in a hurry to reach objectives; not establishing enough time for relationships to develop
Revealing too much too soon (or too little too late) about personal struggles

there's Ishmael, who sees the hopes of his inheritance threatened by his half-brother, Isaac. Rather than navigating the threat, Ishmael mocks Isaac and is driven away. Or Jacob, who doesn't appear to understand his second wife's feelings about being barren, even though his first wife isn't barren and happens to be her sister. And there's also Laban, who mishandles his relationship with his son-in-law Jacob by cheating him for years, only to lose his flocks to him in the end.

Sadly, we are no different today. It would be nice to think we've made a lot of progress by now, but we haven't. Fortunately, there are ways we can work on improving our emotional intelligence. And we also

Table 1.3. Domains of Emotional Intelligence

Primary domains of emotional intelligence	Question to ask to learn about or grow in this domain	Biblical example of high emotional intelligence in this domain
Knowing one's own emotions	What am I feeling?	Hannah (1 Samuel 1:1-18) David (2 Samuel 6:7-12) Job (Job 23) Father of prodigal son (Luke 15:11-24)
Managing emotions	What choice do I want to make about how I will respond to this emotion?	Joseph (Genesis 45:1-5) Daniel (Daniel 3:13-30) Jesus (Mark 11:15-17)
Motivating oneself	What obstacles or frustrations could prevent me from accomplishing my objectives?	Jacob (Genesis 29:15-30) Moses (Exodus 17:1-7, 18) Nehemiah (Nehemiah 6)
Recognizing emotions in others	What is the other person feeling?	Joseph (Genesis 40:7-8) King Artaxerxes (Nehemiah 2:1-8) Jesus (John 8:43-50, Luke 19:1-10)
Handling relationships	How do I want to serve and lead others?	Joseph (Genesis 39:1-5, 46-57) Nathan (2 Samuel 12) Esther (Esther 3, 4 and 5) Jesus (Matthew 20:25-28)

have many stories in the Bible of high emotional intelligence—people who can teach us a lot about how emotional intelligence leads to wisdom, good choices, favor with others, spiritual growth and success. (See table 1.3.)

WHERE AM I NOW?

Volumes of books have been written to help people develop self-awareness. There's so much out there that it's hard to be selective, to find what is helpful and what will give us a well-rounded snapshot of who we are and of our blind spots. And yet knowing who we are only gets us halfway there. Since all of us are people in process, we also need to know *where* we are. If we have all of the knowledge in the world about *who* we are, we will still feel disoriented if we lack knowledge of *where* we are in our journey.

DO THIS

In which of the five domains of emotional intelligence (see table 1.3) do you most want to grow? Read the Scripture recommendations associated with each and answer the questions in the second column as you believe that biblical figure would have. Put yourself in his or her shoes. Once you've increased your level of comfort in that domain, use this activity with your small group.

JENN

A FRIEND AND COLLEAGUE FIRST EXPOSED ME to the concept of spiritual landscapes during a mountain retreat. I was familiar with certain landscape terms: "So-and-so is in the desert," or "It was a mountaintop experience." I had been through the spiritual highs and lows implied in these terms and found them pretty self-descriptive: the desert being a desolate and bleak place where God seems far away, and the mountaintop being an exciting and joyous place where God seems really close. But when he asked me to put landscape language to where I was spiritually at the time, I didn't have the words. Then my friend suggested the plains. He explained it as the place we spend the majority of our time as we journey; we are neither high nor low spiritually. These are the times where we're dealing with a lot of routine, day-in and day-out kind of stuff. Work. Dinner. Dishes. Sleep. The plains resonated.

They may sound a bit dull at first, but then I thought of it as more of an even-keeled and everyday life, a breather. And the category helped me understand why my relationship with God didn't seem as exciting as it once had. Or why I wasn't clinging to him for survival like I used to. Was I out of step with him? Was I doing something to cause a separation between us? No, I was just in a normal part of the journey—the plains. And that was freeing to recognize. It opened me up to considering what God had for me right here rather than trying to get back to something I had once experienced.

This type of knowledge has helped me tremendously when dealing with my clients and people I encounter in my leadership role at church. The awareness helps me meet people where they are and try to serve to them there. Rather than trying to help them get out of the desert, I've attempted to try to help them engage with it to fully experience where God has them. Or, in order to have more empathy or patience, I try to recall how the landscape they are in has been important to my spiritual journey. People definitely respond better to this than the performance-driven solutions we often hear in Christian communities: "Perhaps if you would pray more diligently you might not be in this place" is not typically a helpful response, while a discussion about how hard it is to wander in the desert, hoping for an oasis, often is.

We've only scratched the surface of knowing ourselves. There are so many resources out there to help us develop as small group facilitators and in our personal journeys. And more often than not, those paths of development are directly linked. The better we know ourselves the more we will grow as facilitators. (We have some resources listed at the end of the book.)

"For now we see only a reflection as in a mirror; then we shall see face to face. Now I know in part; then I shall know fully, even as I am fully known" (1 Corinthians 13:12).

EXERCISES AND REFLECTION QUESTIONS

Exercise

Once you have a general idea of your values, complete the values-clarification exercise in appendix three and establish a prioritized list of your values. With each of your top five values, ask yourself, *How much is this value being honored in my small group now?* Make a commitment to do three things this week that will increase satisfaction in the three lowest-rated areas. Journal about what you notice.

Going deeper. Take your list of values and dig deeper to see if there is a core meaning related to each value by completing this statement repeatedly until you get to the core: I value _____ (name the value) because _____ (its impact). Examples: I value meaningful relationships because they lead to intimacy. I value intimacy because I long to know and be known. I long to know and be known because I believe we are created in the image of Christ. I long to know Christ. Core value = knowing Christ.

Reflection Questions

1. What are some of your peak experiences as a facilitator? What does the answer to this question reveal about your strongest values in facilitating a small group?

2. What are some values or motives you have concerns about or perhaps are trying to disown?

3. What are your triggers or biases? What are the emotions that accompany them?

4. Think of a recent emotion you experienced in your small group and how you responded. How do you hope to respond to this emotion the next time you experience it?

5. Using the material in this chapter as a framework, how do some of

the differences between yourself and those in your group play themselves out?

6. What are some concrete ways you draw out the strengths of those
   in your group and honor the ways in which they are different from
   you?

7. How would you describe your current spiritual landscape? Do you
   resist or embrace this place? What will you do to more intentionally
   engage with where God has you?

2

CHARTING THE COURSE

Stages of Group Life

There is a time for everything,
and a season for every activity
under the heavens:

> *a time to be born and a time to die,*
> *a time to plant and a time to uproot,*
>
> *a time to kill and a time to heal,*
> *a time to tear down and a time to build,*
>
> *a time to weep and a time to laugh,*
> *a time to mourn and a time to dance.*

ECCLESIASTES 3:1-4

Remember the old flannel-graph story of Moses leading the people of Israel out of Egypt? Flaming foliage and walls of water? Let's look at the process of how that group of people came together through some truly bizarre shared experiences. And if you want to feel better about yourself as a facilitator, just imagine the people of Israel as Moses' group members.

Right off the bat Moses is a little conflicted about leading these people. Even before he met them, he had concerns. And when he did meet them, his concern seemed pretty well-founded. The people could be described initially as "resistant." Apparently, they hadn't gotten God's memo that Moses was in charge. However, after the whole ten plagues thing, they were willing to listen. They did what he told them—took the jewelry from the Egyptians and ran. When the Red Sea parted, it seemed things were off to a good start.

But the honeymoon didn't last forever. The quarreling and complaining started up around the same time that they hit the desert. "Where's the water?" "Where's the meat?" "We had it better back in Egypt." And on and on. After the people got mad and Moses got mad and God got mad, they eventually negotiated a truce. True, the truce involved lots and lots of dead quail, but it was a truce nonetheless.

And then things started moving forward. Moses was obviously the leader and the people began respecting that leadership. They organized. They found ways to settle internal disputes. They established tribes, clans, rules, structure, systems and a tabernacle. Under a new leader, Joshua, their productivity turned outward. They entered the land God had promised them, even though it was scary. They divided it up and helped each other settle. They reached their goal of becoming an independent nation. Then they renewed their covenant with God.

The children of Israel essentially went through the stages of group life. Groups have a natural life cycle. Moses' group may sound a bit daunting, but the good news is this: probably it won't take forty years for your group cycle through the stages.

In chapter one we talked about self-awareness as a facilitator, how important it is to understand ourselves, where we are and what's required of us right now. Let's take that to the group level. A lack of awareness about where the group is in its life cycle is an under-recognized obstacle to health. We end up lacking direction, lacking an understanding of both where we are and where we're trying to go. Our assumption in this chapter is that groups are all in different places. They have a natural life cycle and travel along it at different paces.

It's good to hear about what's going on in groups other than your own. Sometimes small group facilitators hang out with other group facilitators, both formally and informally. There are parties, facilitator meetings, church services and the like. One of the best things about those kinds of connections—other than the awesome parties you'll be invited to—is being able to exchange stories and hear about each others' experiences. At our church, and some other churches we know of, we have quarterly facilitator dinners, a chance for groups of five to seven facilitators to come together for the express purpose of sharing stories with each other: spiritual explorers attending and finding something different in this community, people growing deeper in their faith by taking steps to stretch themselves, stories of reliance on God when people come to the end of themselves, new realizations about Scripture that open eyes to new ways of living.

Well, sometimes you'll hear wonderful stories about how terrific small groups are. Other times you'll hear stories about Christians acting cliquish, as if they're back in junior high school, or stories of conflict, infighting and power struggles, or no real stories at all, just a recent history of no shows and general malaise. That's not as fun. But one of the more difficult combinations is when someone else is telling stories in the first category and you're telling stories in the second. At times like that it's easy to start doubting yourself. *What's wrong with me that my group isn't going as well as their group?* A subtle but damaging sense of competition can begin to creep in.

One relevant category becomes helpful here: life stages of a group. So often as facilitators we think of small groups as little machines that chug along at exactly the same pace forever, finishing one study and picking up a new one (unless something goes horribly wrong and the machine blows apart). In general, if you put in the right raw material and do regular oil changes, you get predictable results.

That understanding of groups would be a lot simpler, and certainly easier to manage, but the problem is it's just not true. When we're working with real live human beings, nothing is ever as simple or as uniform as that. Our groups, like ourselves, are much messier and more up-and-down. We get in bad moods. We stake out our turf and fight with each other. We have trouble understanding those who are different than ourselves. Groups are not like machines. They are much more organic than that.

It's no accident that we've used the image of a river. A river, although not strictly speaking alive, seems to have a life of its own. It has a starting point, along with various stages and speeds along its path. And then the river ends. Some rivers have longer courses than others. Some branch out into more than one stream, some run into the ocean, and others gradually slow during dry seasons and allow their water to be absorbed into the thirsty ground. But all rivers end somewhere.

Knowing where we are in the river's course—the life stage of the group—helps us better understand what's going on and what's needed. When we have a broader perspective, we can see specific group issues we're dealing with in their larger context. Listen to these struggles shared by small group facilitators:

> I guess I'm feeling a little frustrated. When I started this group a couple months ago, I had envisioned it going deeper, people really sharing what's going on in their hearts. But it just seems like people aren't opening up. We've still got too many "my aunt's having surgery" prayer requests, and too many "So what do you do for a living?" questions. It's really boring. This sounds kind of bad, but do the people in the group just lack depth?

Everything seemed to have gotten off to a good start when the group first started meeting. People had gotten to know each other, and things were going along fine. Then all of a sudden people started asking questions about the direction of the group. We already covered all of that at the beginning. I'm not sure why they're feeling the need to rehash it. Some of the more vocal members are challenging what I'm doing and even seem to be trying to take over. Trey suggested that we study something different, and Jessie thinks we should structure the evening differently. It really bothers me that they seem to be implying that I don't know what I'm doing.

We used to be such a great group. We had parties all the time and did service projects together. We were inviting new people and the group was growing. But now it just seems to be fizzling. James is moving away—he got a great position with a ministry in Seattle. Jasmine and Steve got married and now they want to start a couples' group. Ray is too involved with his other activities—he tutors kids and coaches soccer. It just seems like most of the people are heading in other directions. I feel like I must have done something wrong. I guess at this point I should just let the group die a quiet death.

Each of these quotes comes from a facilitator whose group is in a different life stage, in these cases a stage that the facilitator is struggling with. Many of the "problems" that arise in small groups may not be problems at all but natural manifestations of a life stage. That doesn't mean nothing needs to be done—the facilitator usually still needs to intervene, but it's not always the kind of intervention we might initially think.

THE LIFE STAGES OF SMALL GROUPS

Groups are different from each other, but they often follow a general course that facilitators can use to anticipate and prepare for coming changes. Just as babies go through different stages of development as they move toward adulthood, and just as people mature in Christ over time, groups also move through developmental stages.

These are the basic stages of group life:

- *Gathering.* So what are we here for?
- *Negotiating.* So who's in charge? And how do I fit in?
- *Momentum.* Things are rolling.
- *Serving.* Making a difference.
- *Closure.* Time to move on.

GATHERING

Defining the group's purpose. At the gathering stage, people aren't committed to the group yet. They're checking it out, kicking the tires, asking questions. Like the people of Israel watching Moses' negotiations with Pharaoh, they are seeing how it's going. The questions may not be verbalized, but people are asking, Do I want to be part of this? So what are we here for? What's this going to be like? What's the point of the group really going to be? Generally people are playing it safe during this stage, being polite to each other and looking to the facilitator for direction. The escape hatch is still open. If the facilitator doesn't give enough direction at this point, potential members just disappear. After all, they aren't in charge, they're not sure what's supposed to be happening, and as far as they can tell, nothing is happening. Well-meaning facilitators can absolutely kill a group at this point—simply by not taking the reigns.

In my work as a small groups pastor, I talked with a lot of new group facilitators who were just entering the gathering stage. When I started asking them specific questions about what they wanted their groups to be about, this is one of the most common answers: "I just want to create a community. It doesn't much matter what it's about or what the topic is. I think once we get the people there, we'll just see what everyone wants to do."

○   ○   ○

The response to Tara's questions is an admirable sentiment and eminently well-intended, but it virtually never works. First there's the problem of getting people there in the first place. An invitation to this group sounds like a pitch for *Seinfeld:* "It's a group about nothing." Appealing, huh? Then if you do manage to get some people assembled in a living room, try asking them, "So what do you think we should do? What do you want this group to be about?" and listen to the ear-shattering silence. Even with a group of intelligent people who know how to take initiative, you'll get silence. Why? It just feels rude to take over. And that's what it feels like to a new person (and they're all new at this point): taking over.

Also, some people might think the facilitator is being a bit flippant or hasn't taken the time to think through what the group should be about. Facilitators would do well to spend some time in prayer before starting the group, seeking God's direction. The potential impact on the lives of those involved is too significant to be taken lightly. After all, small group leaders are frontline pastors—frontline pastors who often don't have formal training or much experience pastoring. Our attempts to be obedient to God and depend on him—qualities that imply commitment to prayer—are the best and strongest resources we have. The facilitator's reliance on God in prayer should provide some direction for the group.

Sometimes facilitators hear this "take charge" advice as a mandate to be a dictator: don't listen to what anyone else wants—just tell everyone what's going to happen! That's not what we're saying. But at this stage people need to be told something, or there's no starting point. The facilitator will need to give the new group some initial direction, striking a balance between taking charge and letting things happen organically.

Here's something we heard one facilitator say during an initial meeting:

> Now you probably all read the description of the group in the bulletin before coming tonight, so you know it's a study about the Gospel of Mark. But I just want to go over the basics to make sure we're all on the same page. I've spent some time praying about what this group could look like, and although I don't have crystal-clear specifics, I'd like to see us study Mark in a way that feels safe for spiritual explorers. People at any stage of faith are welcome here, but we'll be gearing our conversation mostly toward people who are newer to the faith or who have been

away from church for a while and want a refresher. So we're going to try to avoid jargon and any other technical kind of language. No one will be whipping out the Greek, okay? I'd really like to see us strike a good balance between reading and understanding the story of Jesus and talking about the real life impact—how does reading this affect us, change us, challenge us? How can we engage with the text in a real-life way? So we'll eventually be getting into our own lives as well as the Gospel of Mark. But so much for what I'm thinking. I'd love to hear from the rest of you too. What are you hoping for from this group?

Some general guidelines have been laid down, and the question for the group has been narrowed from "What do you want this group to be about?" to "What do you hope for from this group?" A very different question, but still one that is open-ended enough to allow people to express wishes and desires about the direction of the group. Answers could range from "I'm just hoping to make some friends and get to know some people" to "I'm hoping maybe we could eventually do some service projects together." If the facilitator had asked, "What do you want this group to be about?" the first answer would have sounded bland, possibly even needy, while the second answer would have sounded like an attempt at taking over the agenda. Far from shutting down the ideas and input of others, laying out some general parameters actually provides enough context to allow a freer expression of ideas.

We're off to a good start, but we need to remember that the gathering stage doesn't begin and end the first night a group meets. That may be the initial conversation, but over the next few weeks or even months, people will be watching to see what direction the group really is going. What does the actual purpose of the group seem to be? What values do I see here? Do they match what was stated? In essence, how well does the real-life experience of the group match up to the description agreed upon that first night?

One small group really valued fun during their gathering stage. They turned things usually considered work, like helping someone move, into a big party. There was rarely a shortage of help because of the guarantee of a good time. And they went to great lengths to celebrate birthdays—the "come as a character from *Saturday Night Live*" party was one of the funniest. They went on a camping trip to the mountains. Many of the people in the group would meet regularly during the week for casual get-togethers, like happy hour or football. And they played practical jokes on each other too. Two friends once placed a "for sale by owner" sign in the front yard of a third friend when he was out of town for the weekend—and listed his cell number on the sign.

Remember the information in the last chapter on values? Here's one of the first places it comes into play. Know the values you as a facilitator are bringing into the group. To whatever degree possible, use those values to set clear expectations for the group.

A facilitator named Isaac placed a high value on community ownership of the group. Before the group started, he envisioned group members volunteering to lead the discussion, host, bring the snacks and plan parties. He certainly envisioned regular attendance and a phone call if a "regular" couldn't make it that night.

At first the group seemed to be going well to Isaac. After all, people were just in the getting-to-know-each-other stage. They seemed to be hitting it off, making friends. But somehow, even after several months, the group never seemed to make it to the "ownership" stage. People came on the nights they felt like coming. No one volunteered to facilitate, even when Isaac told them he had to be out of town.

DO THIS

Maintain a list of the values that your group shares collectively (use the list from appendix two to get ideas). Refer back to this list when suggesting curriculum, books, service opportunities and activities.

What was wrong? Why weren't they helping with the running of the group? Why should Isaac have to do everything himself?

Although there were several contributing factors, one significant reason was that Isaac had never directly communicated those expectations and values to the group. He was a very intuitive person, used to picking up on the subtleties, and he assumed that other people in the group would understand and share his vision of what it means to be a good group—after all, isn't it obvious? So he couldn't figure out why they seemed to be actively thwarting that vision. Were they just passive-aggressive? But if you had asked some of the regular attendees, "Hey, how come you didn't call Isaac when you knew you had to miss group?" you'd have been met with a look of confusion. They had no idea that was an expectation. Likewise, when Isaac said he had to be out of town, they took it as synonymous with an announcement that group would be cancelled next week.

The moral of the story? Don't assume your values and vision are the same as everyone else's. Awareness and expression of values and expectations—yours and others'—in the context of the group create the primary foundation for the gathering stage. Those values and expectations, once they are both stated and lived out, will form the basic DNA of the group that guides it for the rest of its lifespan.

JENN

I RECENTLY VISITED A GROUP THAT I HAD BEEN A PART OF in the past. Two or three years had passed since I'd been there, and in that time the group had gotten new facilitators and the majority of the attenders were now unfamiliar to me. Yet I was astonished at how similar the group felt. Even composed of different people, the group had the same vibe. How could that have happened? It had similar strengths and similar struggles. I even recognized the pattern of the evening and certain group rituals. I guess that's the power of DNA— what's planted there in the beginning is there to stay, unless there's a major attempt at overhaul.

○   ○   ○

MAJOR TASK OF THE GATHERING STAGE

Trust. There's one more question people are asking that we must address in the gathering stage. In fact, it's what allows us to move into the next stage of group development. That question is, "Is this a safe place?" Now it's the very beginning of the group. So far everyone is still just being polite, so it's hard to tell. We all want to be liked. So let's lay off the politics, not venture an opinion, wait and see what happens. The problem is—nothing happens until someone decides to take a risk. In order to assess whether or not something is safe, we need to see a risk taken and observe the response. Like a bridge over a chasm, you can't tell for sure if it will hold until someone steps on it. Then you can watch and see whether the bridge collapses or strains under the weight.

Now, surprise, surprise. Guess who gets to step on the bridge first? That's right, the facilitator. If one of the values we want to see expressed in the group is honesty and vulnerability about struggles, we'll need to be the first to take that risk. In the gathering stage, others are looking to the facilitator for cues on the appropriate level of sharing. If we share a very impersonal prayer request, others will follow suit. But if we risk and share a real struggle, we may start to see others come out from behind the curtains too. It may take a while, but modeling is the only way to ensure the presence of most values.

Honest dialogue and risk-taking is what will eventually allow a small group to move past the polite, nonthreatening chitchat of gathering into the next stage of development: negotiating.

WE ASKED SOME FACILITATORS WHAT THEY LEARNED MOST DURING THE GATHERING STAGE:

"We could have saved a lot of time—and grief—later on by developing a statement at the beginning about why we existed and what we could expect of each other."

"Open discussions and setting expectations is really important in this area. I thought people would just catch on as we went. But really, it wasn't fair of me to assume that everyone would just intuitively pick up on where I was going with the group."

NEGOTIATING

So who's in charge? And how do I fit in? Negotiating can sometimes be a euphemism for arguing, yelling or conflict. Or, in the case of Israel, quarrelling. Probably a good share of our readers just felt a knot in their stomach even reading the title of this section. No one enjoys conflict. (Well, almost no one. We have met a few.) But negotiating is actually a bit different than conflict per se. Conflict can happen at any stage of group life. We've devoted all of chapter five to conflict, so you can wait until then to get truly stressed.

DO THIS

During the life of your small group, regularly ask the group this question: "What do you see as being the purpose of our group?"

Negotiating is more like the time in a group meeting when people sit down and get arranged. Who's getting the comfy seat? Who's sitting by whom? Who's off to the side where they can't really see? People want to know their role in the group. They begin testing each other. What if I do this? What will you do then? To what degree is my voice heard? Am I stronger than you? Do I need to take over in this group? Who's really running it? What does the facilitator expect from the rest of us? Who's responsible for the success of the group? What kind of behavior is okay, and what isn't?

When we run into difficulty in the negotiating stage, we can take comfort in the fact that many people in the Bible—not just the Israelites—dealt with it too. Apparently, negotiating was an essential foundation of the church, so we shouldn't be surprised when we run into it in our small groups. Barnabas was a mentor of the apostle Paul. When Paul couldn't convince the apostles to trust him after his conversion (after all, Paul's preconversion life included killing Christians), Barnabas was the one who stood up for him and ran interference with the other apostles. Later they ministered together for a year in Antioch, then began traveling together on missionary journeys. After many adventures, trials and brushes with death, they had a close relationship. Yet we still read this in Acts 15:36-41:

> Some time later Paul said to Barnabas, "Let us go back and visit the be-
> lievers in all the towns where we preached the word of the Lord and see
> how they are doing." Barnabas wanted to take John, also called Mark,
> with them, but Paul did not think it wise to take him, because he had
> deserted them in Pamphylia and had not continued with them in the
> work. They had such a sharp disagreement that they parted company.
> Barnabas took Mark and sailed for Cyprus, but Paul chose Silas and
> left, commended by the believers to the grace of the Lord. He went
> through Syria and Cilicia, strengthening the churches.

Over a disagreement, they parted company. Yet separately, with new
partners, they continued to further the growth of the church, even
more than they would have done had they stayed together. We know
that Paul and John Mark eventually reconciled, implying that Paul and
Barnabas had reconciled as well. Later Paul, writing his second letter to
Timothy, sent greetings that included this request, "Only Luke is with
me. Get Mark and bring him with you, because he is helpful to me in
my ministry" (2 Timothy 4:11).

However, even in cases where there is no reconciliation or mutual
agreement, God can use negotiating situations to accomplish his purposes. Countless new churches have been started that never would
have without a disagreement of some kind with another church. Admittedly, church splits are not good, but God often uses them to create
two growing congregations where before there was only one.

On an interpersonal level—the level we see in small groups—
everyone handles the negotiating stage differently. Due to differing
personalities, some people become more silent during this stage of
group development while others may talk more in an attempt to exert
control. In one group the arrival of the negotiating stage was heralded
by one member beginning to talk. And talk. And talk. Liz spoke freely
about whatever opinions were on her mind: political, interpersonal,
theological. It didn't really matter. She stated her position without a
lot of sensitivity to the fact that other people in the group had different

opinions on those topics. And Liz freely gave people unsolicited advice and issued blanket statements about what the group "should" be doing. And she spoke with a level of informality, shall we say, that some other members of the group found rather off-putting.

At that point, the facilitators had a choice: were they going to let Liz run the group? If they did, they instinctively knew it would be the death knell. Soon no one would be coming back. So they decided to retake the hill. They began by gently trying to redirect the group's conversation. That proved ineffective. So they talked to Liz outside of group. She agreed to change her behavior, but then didn't. Habits can be hard to break.

DO THIS

Be proactive. Once a month (or however often you deem necessary), wrap up the discussion a little early and ask people to share what's going well with the group and what they're hoping for next. This exercise can be especially helpful during the negotiating stage.

So they talked with her again, and together the two cofacilitators and Liz agreed on a strategy. They had permission to interrupt her during group meetings and redirect the conversation. Repeatedly, if necessary. Sometimes she still talked too much or tried to take over. But the important thing was what happened in the other members of the group—they could see the facilitators taking initiative. So they relaxed. The issue, although not entirely resolved, was being dealt with.

Many negotiating issues stem directly from the gathering stage. When gathering hasn't been handled well or clearly enough, confusion abounds and people are more likely to feel insecure during the negotiating stage. They don't know what the rules are, and that makes them uncomfortable.

JENN

ALTHOUGH WORK TEAMS ARE DIFFERENT than small groups in several ways, going through life stages is one thing they have in common.

When I worked in a corporate role at a start-up company, I was a member of a national human resources (HR) team formed to improve HR services and processes. One woman in the group was appointed as the team leader and then was subsequently slammed by other work-related responsibilities for the next few months. Because of a perceived lack of leadership, we experienced some intensified negotiating. People were unsure of their roles and either did or didn't want to take over—and there was no agreement on what was appropriate. Little progress was being made on our tasks.

During our next off-site meeting, the leader took us through a simple exercise that was very helpful. She asked us each to respond to two questions: What do you like best about how our team has functioned? What do you need next from this team? I thought these questions were brilliant because they kept us focused on building from the positive experiences and also reduced the amount of finger pointing that may have taken place.

The team agreed that it needed a leader who could be more engaged in the process of managing projects. Due to the initial leader's time constraints, I was appointed to take over the role even though I was far less qualified. Once that transition took place, everyone noticed that the tension had subsided. Through this experience, I learned about the importance of *communication* during the negotiating stage. When people are given a chance to publicly share what they desire for the group, they are more capable of getting unstuck and reengaging with the purpose of the group.

A regular practice of the facilitator should be listening to the prompting of the Holy Spirit. And negotiating is a particularly critical time in group development to do so. Many of the questions group members are asking are underground at this stage, so a great deal of discernment on the part of the facilitator is required. Are things going along as smoothly as it seems? Are the group members' values being honored? Where is the presence of God being felt? How are others experiencing the group? How could you find ways to help them express any concerns or questions they might have?

Sometimes during the negotiating stage the group realizes they missed the mark during the gathering stage and that the Holy Spirit is calling them to something different—usually bigger. In these situations, people generally feel a sense of disappointment: "This isn't what I thought it would be." At times like these, even when there is no overt disagreement or conflict, it can be helpful to create a space for people to air their feelings, concerns and desires. And sometimes that can shift the direction of the group, effectively creating a regathering during the negotiating stage.

The negotiating stage is where many groups get stuck. Fearing any disagreement, they stay at the pseudo-community stage of being friendly, but not reaching authentic community. Negotiating will lead to either a retreat to pseudo-community, break-up or recommitment, allowing compromise and authentic community. Most groups don't last long enough to survive conflict, so many groups remain superficial, which results in the common feeling that small groups are a waste of time.

To move on from the negotiating stage and into the momentum stage, risk taking and listening are necessary. Listening involves both listening to God and to others. Facilitators need to ask questions that will bring the issues to the surface, and then create an environment for people to be heard. People *need* to feel heard during the negotiating stage.

TARA

DO YOU REMEMBER THE LAST TIME YOU had an argument to present, a point to make or a concern to express, and someone really listened to you? I remember. I was concerned about a policy issue at our church, a change that was being made. It was not a personal issue, but the kind of issue that people can easily begin to feel defensive about. I talked to the appropriate staff person, and instead of becoming defensive, he kept listening and asking me questions. I felt listened to—really listened to without feeling judged or like he was just waiting for me to take a breath so he could make his point or try to move me in a different direction—and I really started to relax. I could feel the tension of a potentially difficult situation drain away. Even though he didn't agree with me, he listened well enough that I felt I didn't have to convince him. He'd heard me enough to understand my concerns. And that was all I really needed. I then felt not only free to move toward problem-solving but also motivated to do so.

MAJOR TASK OF THE NEGOTIATING STAGE

Risk. People need to feel heard in their small groups. They need to feel that their opinions are validated and respected, even if not agreed with. And the facilitator must take the initiative in that. It's much harder for a group member to bring up a difficult topic or a problem

WHAT DID SOME FACILITATORS REMEMBER MOST FROM THE NEGOTIATING STAGE?

"The vibe needs to be consonant with what we are actually saying and doing. People will be able to pick up on the inconsistencies. In our group, we'd talk a lot about being sensitive to those who are spiritual explorers, but we were using language they couldn't understand and not inviting new people or developing relationships with non-Christians. It became a real problem, and finally someone in the group challenged me on it."

"I really should have addressed the problem more directly when a group member started trying to take over too much. I could tell other people in the group were uncomfortable, but I didn't want to be rude and wasn't sure how to address it."

they're having with something than it is for the facilitator to ask questions, ask for feedback and draw others out. Even if there is the risk of disagreement, we need to give people the chance to say what's really on their minds and be heard.

MOMENTUM

Things are rolling. Generally, momentum is the stage of group life that most facilitators are shooting for. When we see the Israelites establishing structure and systems, we know things are moving along. We know where we're meeting, who's going to be there, what time people will arrive and what time we'll start the discussion. We understand our roles in the group. We can good-naturedly roll our eyes at each other's foibles and characteristic traits. *There Anthony goes again with one of his silly puns. Looks like Lindsey has found another opportunity to talk about the importance of thinking for oneself—again.*

We met with one pastor to ask him various questions about the impact of small groups at his church. He paused for a moment, and then with great enthusiasm said, "Let me tell you about *my* small group!" He came alive as he shared about this group that formed just a couple of years ago and had reached the momentum stage. He was proud of the group—about their interactions and discussions, the caring and loving community they'd developed, and the challenges they made it through together. Even listening to the stories created a sense of, *Wow. I want to be part of a group like this.* Over and over—even when he was talking about a couple they'd "taken in" after an affair or the spiritual abuse they were helping a member overcome—you could tell the group was having a good time together. "We never stopped having fun together—even in crisis," the pastor shared. "We've even gone on vacation together. That was a great time."

DO THIS

Groups that have fun together are the most successful small groups. Be intentional about having fun together.

Yes, things were moving along comfortably for this group. But the thing to watch for at the momentum stage is whether things are moving along *too* comfortably.

The dangers at this stage of group life are some of the most subtle. Some facilitators may notice an increase in inward focus at this stage. Members stop inviting new people—it's "us four and no more." Other facilitators deal with stagnation: we're into our comfortable routine, but that comfort eventually turns to boredom. Nothing new or interesting is happening. Wouldn't it feel better to stay home and watch the game tonight?

So a facilitator's challenge at this point is to keep adding fresh energy to the group. This energy can take the form of new people (assuming the group is an open one) or new activities. In the case of the Israelites, a new leader was prepared to take the group to the next stage.

A Bible study group was working through the Old Testament. They had been meeting diligently for two years, learning their stories and history, laughing together, and praying for one another. The group had a very committed core of people attending. One way the facilitator kept the group interesting and fresh during the momentum stage, which lasted a long time in this group, was that every time the group finished a book of the Bible, they took a week off to have a party. Each time the party was different—different locations, different people planning it. But it kept the elements of relationship and fun going strong in the group.

DO THIS

Spend one gathering discussing where everyone sees the group in a year (or three years). This exercise can be especially helpful during the momentum stage.

MAJOR TASK OF THE MOMENTUM STAGE

Belonging. A couples' group in the momentum stage decided they needed some fresh blood even though they were a closed group. They decided once a month to sponsor a "meet new friends night." The group would host a dinner party and each couple would invite a friend or two. It wasn't part of the group meeting per se, but it helped the group retain an outward focus and opened up avenues for meeting new people. Over time, the group began using "meet new friends night" as a way to reach out to neighbors and coworkers who didn't yet know Christ. This story illustrates the movement of a group from the momentum stage into the serving stage. Momentum provides the foundation for serving— mission born out of authentic community. Serving then goes on to fulfill the desire for impact and significance.

SERVING

Making a difference. Sometimes when people think of what takes place in small groups, they think of "fellowship" or, worse yet, "being fed." Thus serving would be the opposite: now that you've been fed, leave the safe house, go out and give to others. But it's not taking in versus giving out. Ideally, they're done at the same time. Why not serve, but do so out of a relational context? Why not bring it all together?

With small groups, serving is about having a mission to accomplish outside of the group. Some groups, especially groups formed with a missional purpose, will start serving others right from the

WHAT DID OUR FACILITATORS
REMEMBER MOST FROM THE MOMENTUM STAGE?

"That stage felt like the Golden Age of our group. I only wish I had used that time more to visioncast for the future instead of assuming that it would continue indefinitely."

"Things were going fine, but our time together started feeling pretty stale. We knew exactly what to expect. It seemed like we were making the same prayer requests and talking about the same old things. I was afraid to address it, and I think my not addressing it is what led to the group petering out. We needed to be challenged to go in new directions."

beginning. But other groups reach this stage almost by accident. They have had a great run and start feeling prompted by the Spirit to move outward, to serve in some way. The deepening relationships, instead of becoming ingrown, create a unity that results in broader impact.

We talked to a member of one small group that formed nearly thirty years ago. This couples' group came together after ten marriages in their close-knit community fell apart due to infidelity. They formed to "protect and encourage" their marriages, but the couples were all also involved in the same parachurch ministry that shared a commitment to helping teenagers.

When asked what the group does when they are together, the woman laughed and said, "We have never in twenty-eight years made it through a book. We've really tried, but something always gets in the way. When we get together, we talk, pray and have fun." She talked about a cruise they all went on for their twenty-fifth anniversary as a group—including a couple that had moved out of state ten years before the anniversary. She talked about their families camping together and attending annual Christmas parties.

DO THIS

As your group matures, try simple ways of changing the dynamic, such as meeting in a different location or asking members not to sit beside their spouse.

But she also shared about losing a couple to divorce, helping each other through the death of parents and encouraging each other with challenging parenting issues. Her stories were inspiring, and it was clear she could have talked for hours about the impact of this small group—not only on the lives of these families but also on the teenagers they served together and on the kingdom of God as a whole. Their community together deepened their commitment to ministry.

Serving could almost be described as self-discovery, not just for an individual but for the whole group—a way of reaching out or engaging with the world in a way that stems from the group's identity. Not all groups reach this life stage, but for those that do, the effect can be deep and lasting.

Any good study of Scripture, any good discussion or book or Christian concept or idea, any good relational connection with another follower of Christ is not an end in itself. It was not designed for its own sake. A study of Scripture calls us to something—it calls us to live differently. To take action of some kind. To care for the poor, to engage with the world, to create art or to love the unlovely. Each group must listen for that calling: What is God saying to us? How is he speaking? Where do we hear his voice? What part does he have for us to play in this world?

Three couples had formed a tight-knit small group. They met for years. Eventually, they began wondering if they were too inward-focused. They felt like the time had come for a shift of some kind. All of the couples had small children and shared a passion for investing in the holistic formation of their children—spiritual, behavioral, emotional, physical. Ideas began bubbling and they talked about how to share that passion with others.

Eventually, they formed a nonprofit organization to provide parenting resources and coaching for families. As usually is the case with the body of Christ, they found they all had different gifts they could use to make this nonprofit successful. Curt is on the board, watching over the business and financial end. Lisa and Sophie are doing the direct parent-coaching. Jack put on a fundraiser party so they could share the vision and gain support in the early stages. Each member of this six-member group is using his or her gifts and talents in some way for the good of the whole. And talk about impact; they've now served hundreds of families, some who were at their wits' end, some who did not know Christ.

The beauty of an outward-focused group is difficult to overstate. It's the body of Christ getting its feet and hands dirty, becoming truly incarnate. The sight of that kind of loving, active engagement is rare. It inspires. And those of us who encounter it catch a whiff of the transcendent in the air.

MAJOR TASK OF THE SERVING STAGE

Contributing. One historical example of a small group of believers who made a difference through their outward focus is the Clapham Sect in England at the turn of the nineteenth century. William Wilberforce, who fought for the abolition of slavery, is one of the better-known members, but there were at least eight other influential members of the group involved in matters of public policy. They were all Christians who banded together for like-minded fellowship and fought for social causes. Collectively, the members of the Clapham Sect had far-reaching impact through their work to combat slavery, food shortages, unjust penal laws and the exploitation of children as chimney sweeps. They supported overseas missions and the rise of Sunday school programs for Christian education. The influence of this small group of believers far outstripped their numbers.

DO THIS

Read about the Clapham Sect or watch the movie *Amazing Grace* together. Discuss ways your group could serve others together.

CLOSURE

Time to move on. Jesus' ministry was going strong. He was teaching, healing, gaining more followers. He was making a difference. You can

---

**WHAT DO SOME FACILITATORS
REMEMBER FROM THE SERVING STAGE?**

"There was this great sense of freedom. The group was no longer a group for the sake of being a group. It's almost like it transformed into something else and was serving a wider purpose beyond itself."

"I was kind of scared when we moved into this stage. I thought I might not be up to it, and I was worried I'd miss the community we'd had before. It was really challenging, but I ended up growing significantly through the experience."

imagine the excitement among the disciples at the way things were taking off. The earthly kingdom of God must be just around the corner. Even the Pharisees were saying to one another, "See, this is getting us nowhere. Look how the whole world has gone after him!" (John 12:19).

It was at this particular time that Jesus decided to tell his disciples, "The hour has come for the Son of Man to be glorified. Very truly I tell you, unless a kernel of wheat falls to the ground and dies, it remains only a single seed. But if it dies, it produces many seeds" (John 12:23-24).

Just when things seemed to be at their most fruitful, just when things were really taking off, Jesus apparently decides to call it quits. He starts talking about death—his death. The disbanding of the Twelve. The end. But, as we find in the reading of Acts, the seeds of new beginnings, new endeavors, new eras, are always found in the ashes of the old.

Sometimes people refer to this last stage of group life not as closure but as transformation. That's probably a better word for it because although this life stage involves endings and goodbyes, if a group has called people closer to God, it will also involve new beginnings. Like it did for the Israelites.

Remember the quote from the group leader at the beginning of this chapter? Read it again, this time looking for the seeds of new beginnings:

> We used to be such a great group. We had parties all the time and we did service projects together. We were inviting new people and the group was growing. But now it just seems to be fizzling. James is moving away—he got a great position with a ministry in Seattle. Jasmine and Steve got married and now they want to start a couple's group. Ray is too involved with his other activities—he tutors kids and coaches soccer. It just seems like most of the people are heading in other directions. I feel like I must have done something wrong. I guess at this point I should just let the group die a quiet death.

The biggest mistake this facilitator could make at this point is to let the group die a quiet death. What she should do is celebrate! And be intentional about celebrating. It sounds like the group was of high quality and had a lasting effect, doesn't it? That's something to be celebrated. Look at all of the fruit that resulted from this group: people encouraged as they volunteer in the community, people developing a vision for starting new groups, people moving into new and challenging ministry positions. That's not the death of a group; that's its fruit. The seed that fell to the ground and died is beginning to sprout new life. Often the vision for the next endeavor is found in the embers of the last powerful experience. Following this line of reasoning, the facilitator should consider what the next steps are for her. Far from being a failure, God used her to lead a highly successful group, and she should consider where to go next with those gifts.

Sometimes a group has to die. There are exceptions—one women's prayer group we know of has met for forty years. At this point, they all have to call their daughters for rides and have trouble remembering whose house they're meeting at. But groups of that duration are the exception rather than the rule. Generally, a group runs its course within a few years. And as we have seen, that's not necessarily a bad thing if it has accomplished its purpose.

The bad thing is when facilitators don't provide appropriate closure. Usually when a group ends, the facilitator is dealing with at least some level of shame and discouragement. They feel as if they've failed. And that sense of shame can prevent them from bringing closure to the group.

When a group experience is drawing to a close, members can usually sense it. If the facilitator ignores this next life stage of the group—closure or transformation—members can feel disappointed or abandoned, as if the facilitator is implying that the group's time together meant nothing or has been forgotten. It just fizzles out.

So what is the alternative? Instead of quietly fading away, facilitators can commit to going out with a bang. Throw a party. Celebrate accomplishments. Reminisce. Say goodbye, even if some of the group members will still see each other. Talk about new directions for the future. (Multiplication and starting new groups will be discussed in chapter six.) Focus on the past joy, the current love and the future hope.

A men's group had been instrumental in walking each other through the challenging process of singleness, dating and finally proposing. It had been a closed group with a limit of twelve men who covenanted to meet for one year. The purpose of the group had been to call each other toward courageous and godly behavior as men—which in this case involved the daunting challenge of asking women out. Several of the men struggled with the leap of faith required, but they moved forward and a few had become engaged when the group came to a close.

They decided to celebrate by taking an overnight retreat in the mountains. Around a campfire they shared stories, celebrated and participated in curious male-bonding behaviors such as smack-talk. They also partook in a ritual burning, in which various symbolic items were thrown into the fire. Since women were not privy to this event, we are not sure exactly what kinds of things met a fiery demise, but the ritual certainly lends itself to the imagination. Then they closed the evening with formal words of blessing and encouragement for each member. Now *this* is a group that was intentional about closure. Many of those men—and their wives—have gone on to start new groups and even start new churches.

Celebration is deeply rooted in biblical history. Remember David bringing the ark of the covenant into Jerusalem, dancing before the Lord with all of his might, not worrying about what anyone else was thinking? And whenever there was a momentous event in the Old Testament— an encounter with God—people marked the place by building an altar. When Abraham was traveling and God appeared to him and said, "To your offspring I will give this land," Abraham responded by building an altar there to the Lord (Genesis 12:6-7). Isaac followed suit when God appeared and spoke to him (Genesis 26:24-25). And when Jacob wrestled all night with an angel, the Bible says, "There he built an altar, and he called the place El Bethel, because it was there that God revealed himself to him when he was fleeing from his brother" (Genesis 35:7).

Encounters with God need to be marked. They require a memorial of some kind, a picking of stones and piling them upon one another, a marker to say, "This happened here." Encounters with God in our groups need to be marked, celebrated, remembered.

But what if the group wasn't so great? What if it didn't really take off or went down in flames or fizzled out over time or was below par? Even if things went poorly in some ways, the closure stage is still a time to get together for debriefing. To celebrate the things that did go well (there are always some) and to talk honestly about what didn't go well. This conversation can be really scary for facilitators. The number one reason facilitators do not ask for feedback from group members on how things went is fear. Facilitators generally feel that they are the ones responsible for the group, and therefore everything that didn't go well is their fault. If a facilitator suspects things haven't gone well or met

DO THIS

Consider how to become more missional as a small group. Read books on the topic to discern how to love and serve others better. Invest in a cause together, go on a mission trip together or volunteer regularly serving the poor.

expectations, why ask people about it? How will it help to get people together and talk about?

MAJOR TASK OF THE CLOSURE STAGE

Celebrating. Unfortunately, asking for feedback—daunting as that may be—is one of the ways we grow. We can learn from that feedback and not make the same mistakes twice. A willingness to learn from our mistakes through open, honest dialogue is a mark of integrity and true leadership. A tool for creating dialogue around feedback is found in the table on page 160. You can adapt stage two to gather feedback—this stage is useful for feedback whether or not there is a conflict.

Additionally, we owe it to the people in our groups to provide closure. Especially when things don't go well, people are more likely to fade away into a lack of involvement if they are not drawn out and heard. When things end badly and there is no dialogue, there's not only a lack of closure but often hurt feelings and awkwardness in relationships. And again, the facilitator is the one who needs to initiate potentially difficult dialogues.

Finally, celebrate what did go well even if things are ending poorly. Good things still happened in the midst of it, and it's important to acknowledge them and celebrate the way God worked in us.

ALL WORK AND NO PLAY

Groups do not move through these stages in a linear fashion over a predictable period of time. Some groups stay in one stage longer than others; some move back and forth between stages, sometimes going in reverse or hitting one stage twice. Don't worry—this is normal. One stage isn't any better than the others. There's no "right" place to be. What's important is that the facilitator tries to avoid getting stuck in the stage of his or her comfort zone. Being fully present in each stage while allowing the group to progress will provide the best chance of overall health for the group.

Facilitators seem much more at ease when they know the stage of their group and are able to let the stage be what it is rather than trying to force the group forward or backward to better times. So much can be gained from each stage. A certain level of enjoyment comes from relaxing and letting the group meander its way down the river. We've noticed that the most successful small groups—the ones that are more apt to make it through the bad times—are the ones that really enjoy be-

WHAT DID SOME FACILITATORS REMEMBER FROM THE CLOSURE STAGE?

"I was afraid of the group ending and I have to admit, I didn't really do anything about it. People in the group later told me they felt like they were just standing there alone and everyone was gone."

"I still remember the last time our group met. The words of encouragement spoken to me that night still resonate with me a couple of years later. I had no idea the impact I'd had in some of their lives until they had the opportunity of time set aside to tell me. And I know words of life were spoken to others that night as well."

ing together. They love each other and have fun together at all stages, like many of the groups we've described in this chapter.

All work and no play makes people dull. But the flip side—all play—is not what we're recommending either. For then it becomes something less than a small group—more like a casual gathering of people looking for a good time. And true spiritual growth requires something much deeper than that. A strong group brings together the sacred and the fun and discovers those aren't really as far apart as we often think. A strong group creates a space for people to journey together through the good times, lighten the heaviness of the difficult times, and discover meaning in the routine seasons of life.

EXERCISES AND REFLECTION QUESTIONS

Exercise 1
To ensure you stay focused during each stage of group life, use the following format to create a simple statement that describes the bottom-line reason your group exists: We are a community of _____ (identity) that gather to _____ (impact) and _____ (impact). Example: We are a community of social justice enthusiasts that gather to deepen our relationships with God and consider how to serve international causes.

Exercise 2
First, reflect on the past stage of your small group and (1) list all of the areas in which the group and group members made progress during that season. Celebrate these accomplishments. (2) List all of the disappointments, missed opportunities and regrets.

Second, reflect on what you've learned so far as a facilitator. Choose three to seven of the most important learnings. Examples:

- I learned that silence is powerful.
- I learned that I rely on my own strength more than the power of the Spirit.

Third, write a list of all the goals you want to make progress toward in the next stage of your small group. How do you want to challenge yourself as a facilitator? In what areas do you wish to develop more dependence on God? Consider all of the people in your group. Identify someone you hope will experience a powerful breakthrough in this stage. What can you do for this person?

Reflection Questions

1. Are you clear on the purpose of your small group? Could those attending tell you what the purpose is?

2. What are the values that your group appears to collectively share? What might you do to show respect for those values?

3. What stage is your group in right now? What are the advantages of being in this stage? What are some of the potential dangers of this stage?

4. Do you feel you need to stay where you are right now or move into the next stage? In what ways are you tempted to try to move out of this stage prematurely? In what ways are you tempted to stay in this stage too long?

5. How have your values, emotional intelligence and other leadership attributes influenced the progression of your group through these stages?

6. Having fun together is possible and important at every stage. How will you be more intentional about having fun with your small group this month?

7. How can you assess whether or not your small group has run its course? If it has, how will you end gracefully? If it hasn't, how will you know when it has?

3

EXPLORING THE
UNDERCURRENTS

Listening to God and Others

*The Lord said, "Go out and stand on
the mountain in the presence of the Lord,
for the Lord is about to pass by."*

*Then a great and powerful wind tore
the mountains apart and shattered
the rocks before the Lord, but the
Lord was not in the wind.*

*After the wind there was an earthquake,
but the Lord was not in the earthquake.
After the earthquake came a fire, but the
Lord was not in the fire. And after
the fire came a gentle whisper.*

1 KINGS 19:11-12

Our friend Bruce shared a story with us about an experience he had in
his small group. A group of his friends had been meeting for several
months and had shared some pretty significant stories about their
lives. Bruce was excited to tell them about a conversation he had with

one of his best friends whom the group had prayed for in the past. His friend had emotionally withdrawn from him years before and was going through a difficult time as a result of a DUI, which had caused him to face up to his alcoholism. Bruce shared with the group how he and his friend recently broke through some of the barriers between them and resolved things that had happened in their relationship a long time ago. He told them how he was able to talk to his friend about Christ and how his own life had been affected by returning to his Christian upbringing.

Sharing this story required Bruce to reveal a few things about his life before Christ that elicited a strong sense of shame—about his own DUI and some other choices he was not proud of. He spoke for five or ten minutes, with enthusiasm for his friend and with a bit of awkwardness about his own past, and then wrapped up the story. He looked around the room and was greeted by silence. Ten, thirty, sixty seconds went by. No one said a word. No one looked at him. Another minute went by and the subject was changed—the group went on to a new conversation.

Have you ever experienced this? Been in a small group setting where a member has just bared his or her soul and the group's response was silence? Awkwardness? No eye contact? Perhaps an obligatory, "Thanks for sharing," or some sort of inappropriately placed joke as a misguided attempt to lighten the mood? We've had numerous experiences like this in small groups (and admit that we've been on both ends) and have wondered how to help facilitators navigate these moments—the still waters.

These moments hold a disproportionate amount of power in a group. The still waters have the power to bring deep healing and create awestricken moments of redemption—the kind of moments in which you hold your breath and feel a rising in your chest because you can't believe what you're seeing. Think of Jesus asking, "Who touched me?" and the ensuing silence that came over the crowd. A silence pregnant with possibilities. And a woman having to make a choice. *Do I say something? Do I try to hide?*

But the same moments that hold so much promise also harbor the potential to do serious and lasting damage. It's at these moments that people make critical decisions: Can I trust this group? How much is appropriate to share? Am I cared about? Am I accepted? Do I need to wear the happy-Christian mask? Am I necessary here? Do I matter? And those questions can be answered either way.

Another friend returned to church one Sunday after a prodigal-type experience. After having royally messed up some things in her life, she was terrified to go back to church, fearful of being judged or ignored, of walking into the unknown of people's responses. What would happen in the silence when she saw people who remembered her? They'd be caught unprepared, unready to make a response. What she was asking was, "Will I be accepted again? Is it okay for me to come back?"

DO THIS

Be prepared for those moments where you may be unsure how to respond. Example: "I'm not sure how best to respond, but I want you to know how much I appreciate that you shared your story with us. That took courage. Thanks."

Powerful small group experiences start with truly listening to people, not just hearing their words. The difference between hearing and listening is that listening requires both engagement and response, even though the response may be unspoken. Hearing simply means that words spoken have registered through our ears. Listening, when it involves engagement and response, is simultaneously one of the easiest and most difficult skills to grasp and apply well. Margaret Wheatley, a writer and organization consultant, wrote in her book *Finding Our Way,* "Listening is such a simple act. It requires us to be present, and that takes practice, but we don't have to do anything else. We don't have to advise, or coach, or sound wise. We just have to be willing to sit there and listen. If we can do that, we create moments in which real healing is available." But how can we be sure we're present? And how can we be sure others know we're present?

Most people consider themselves good listeners. Statistics prove otherwise:

- Amount of the time we are distracted, preoccupied or forgetful: 75 percent
- How much we usually recall immediately after we listen to someone talk: 50 percent
- How much we remember later of what we hear: 20 percent (International Listening Association: www.listen.org)

Although we can listen at 125-250 words per minute, we can think at 1,000-3,000 words per minute (HighGain: www.highgain.com), allowing ample time for our minds to drift to unrelated thoughts, move to conclusions about the point being made or formulate our own next comments. As one person put it, "I know you believe you understand what you think I said, but I am not sure you realize that what you heard is not what I meant."

Essentially, most of us think we're good listeners only because we don't have a very clear understanding of what's involved in listening. Think back to Bruce, who shared about his DUI. What are the possibilities? Perhaps people in his group were searching so hard for the "right" thing to say that nothing was said at all. Perhaps they were empathizing, but didn't know how to engage. Perhaps they were afraid of sounding judgmental and so opted to say nothing. Perhaps they were dealing with memories from their own pasts that were interfering with their ability to reach out or even look at him. Perhaps they were thinking all kinds of things, but since they didn't respond, Bruce felt they weren't really listening.

There are many possible reasons for the silence, and Bruce was left to wonder about them. And since Bruce is like most of us, it's no surprise that in lieu of information, he assumed the worst. He said he felt hurt, judged and rejected. He regretted sharing and wished he'd not revealed as much about his own story. Bruce later said, "I felt like the group heard me. They could have recalled the facts of my story, but an important part of what I was really saying was not being listened to, the part that was underneath the words."

Listening goes well beyond hearing the details and facts of what's being said. It involves connecting to the unspoken—the body language and the emotions behind the words. Underneath Bruce's story, he was really asking, "If I am honest about my past, and you know the bad things I've done, will you still accept me?"

Those kinds of conversations require courage—on both sides. Poet David Whyte popularized the phrase "courageous conversations." When asked by HR.com what he meant by courageous conversation, Whyte said,

DO THIS

Ask your group to evaluate how well they believe the group engages in courageous conversations. Ask them to specify a few recent ones. Ask them to discuss their levels of comfort and discomfort with these types of conversations.

> Well, I suppose it's good to go to the root of the word "courage," which comes from the old Norman French "coeur" meaning heart. I suppose a courageous conversation is a heart-felt one. And a heart-felt conversation is one that needs to happen. I often say that a courageous conversation is the one you should be having. (David Whyte, "Thought Leaders" Interview with Karen Elmhirst)

Courageous conversations lead to growth. Which is why they are exactly the kind of conversations we want to have in our small groups. Spiritual growth does not come through safe or polite conversations, but through courageous and risky ones. As Whyte puts it, "If you get into a real conversation, it's going to nourish you, but it will also pull you apart to make way for the new person" ("Thought Leaders"). Sounds like fun, huh? Or maybe more like various torture techniques that have since been made illegal. Growth can certainly be painful. But it helps immensely to have the right people on the journey with you.

We have both been involved at various times in our lives with smaller accountability groups—two or three other women who journey closely with us, take part in our lives, encourage us to draw closer to God, and pray with us. In one of these groups, on a particularly difficult night, a woman was faced with the type of life crisis we pray we never have to experience. She called her friends to come over and help her through the night.

Facing crisis alone is a terrifying prospect. This woman had no family living in the area to call. But what she did have was a group of friends who had been engaged in courageous conversations with her for a couple of years. They knew the details of her past, the ins and outs of her relationships, the many prayers she'd spoken before God. The other women in her group had a pretty good sense of how the crisis might be affecting her and what she might need from them because she had made a decision years ago to invite them into her story.

After hugging and crying together, the events turned into a scene like you might see in a dark comedy cult film as everyone in the group seemed to take on a new persona—the antithesis of who they usually are. The calmest of the group said, "It really seems like it might help to destroy something. Let's slash the sofa cushions." After a pregnant pause and some very startled glances in her direction, the most logical of the group decided she agreed, grabbed a lamp and was about to hurl it across the room (without even unplugging it) when the most emotionally driven of the group got everyone to come to their senses.

That night exposed some of the highs and lows of community. On one hand the group was able to express their love for their friend in such an unconditional way that she did not have to censor herself for them or pretend to feel any differently than she felt. Of course, they did consider recreational drugs as a viable option—briefly. But somehow they managed to make their friend laugh simply by how they were handling (or mishandling) the crisis. Momentary respite from the pain, if only for a few moments one night.

As one of the friends reflected on this story she wondered, *Was I the right person to walk through this crisis with my friend?* She is not sure. Or perhaps it depends on who you ask. Some may feel she broached the topic of forgiveness too soon. However, she'd like to think that somehow by the grace of God all *three* of the friends were, at certain times, the right *person* for their friend. At times she needed the one who helped her to be with her anger. Other times she needed the one who encouraged her to be strong, or the one that wanted her to experience forgiveness.

This crisis and all that's transpired since has led to growth—growth of the torturous variety, of course. The group of friends was forced to engage with the hidden parts of each of them that were angry, fearful or judgmental. Consistent with God's mystery, engaging with those hidden parts somehow led to freedom, and helped them find laughter in other dark moments. When they gathered they often seemed to be creating a new scene for a future play or sitcom or book. Whether lamenting over being single or being married, career opportunities or challenges, family dysfunction, getting older—topics that can feel heavy and overwhelming—they shared many laughs as they made way for new growth in their lives. And they all know who they will call when the life crisis is theirs.

COFACILITATING WITH GOD

No, God is not our copilot. And he is not our coleader, especially if that implies that we are senior-in-command and he is helping us out. In fact, it usually feels more like we are sitting at the wheel (or whatever instrument pilots use) with no idea what to do, the plane going out of control, and we suddenly become all too aware that we absolutely cannot do this. The group and all of its passengers will be going down in flames soon if we cannot tap into some source of power or wisdom that far outstrips our own. We need God. We need prayer. Listening to others in the group when they are speaking is important, but listening to God when he is speaking is essential. Depending on your tradition, you may call that voice intuition, the Holy Spirit, the leading of the Lord or any number of things. But what we mean here is tapping into a spiritual power that is beyond our own resources, reliance on a God who is greater than us.

Our friend Simone had an experience of listening to the Holy Spirit in her group one night. Before the formal discussion had started, while people were still milling around the kitchen, another woman in the group mentioned offhandedly that her father had been unable to provide financially for her family for many years when she was younger. Ashley casually, almost jokingly, referenced the stress and embarrassment that it had caused her growing up. Although it wasn't much more than a sidebar comment, mentioned in passing because it was somehow related to the topic at hand, Simone felt that something deeper was being revealed to her. She noticed a brief flash of pain in Ashley's eyes, and sensed that the wound was deeper than her words and matter-of-fact posture revealed.

DO THIS

Take time to talk one-on-one with people in your group who regularly seem to bring the topic back to themselves. Let them know the impact that behavior might have on others in the group. Ask them to try listening to someone using only reflective listening responses such as "yes," "I see" and "tell me more."

She heard slight inflections in Ashley's voice and recognized the dissonance in her manner. Simone realized she was being prompted by God to pursue Ashley and ask more questions about her father. She followed that prompting and entered into the conversation, and for a moment they were bonded as Simone "got it."

Now, if you knew Simone, this would be an even better story. She's a very matter-of-fact, down-to-earth kind of woman. She has little patience for mysticism and generally takes things at face value. In short, Simone is not someone who would generally pick up on the subtleties. But God was working in her and through her, revealing something she would not have seen on her own. To many people this level of discernment comes naturally because it's a spiritual gift. But for others, discernment comes and goes and requires an intentional connection to what's going on—something that can be learned.

CATEGORIES FOR LISTENING

Me, you and us. The traditional way of assessing whether we are good listeners is to look for some of the skills involved. Many communication books have revealed to us a myriad of listening skills: focusing, summarizing, inviting, unpacking and clarifying. And these are good—we highly recommend using them.

But it doesn't stop there. Good listening moves beneath the surface to what's really going on at deeper levels. What are the emotions? What makes us curious to hear more? When we are really engaged in listening to someone, we hear not only the words they are saying but also the feelings behind them. Exploring those feelings will lead to a heartfelt conversation, in which people feel connected and heard. And usually when people visit or join a small group, that is what they are looking for.

WHEN I WAS GETTING MY CERTIFICATION in coaching, I learned about three levels of listening (I, II and III). Simply stated, each level describes where the listener's attention was focused (explained later). I thought I'd read enough about effective communication over the years that I assumed there wasn't much more to be said about listening. But what they described intrigued me, especially given that what was being described as level III listening was so similar to how I had experienced the Spirit of God. For the purposes of small group interactions, we refer to levels I, II, and III as Me, You, and Us because it makes it easier to remember where the listener's focus is.

Level Me: The focus is completely on the self. It's all about *me.* How is what I am hearing affecting me? What am I going to say next? What do I think the speaker is about to say? How do I feel about this topic? What are my emotions? How will I defend my opinion? As you can probably guess, this level of listening is the least helpful in a small group setting, as it is the most self-centered. Small group leaders who get stuck here are in performance mode. It's easy to get stuck here when we are focused on wondering what others think of us, trying to meet their expectations and looking good. But all of those fears and concerns grow up like weeds to choke a fruitful, intended plant, fostering a powerful, authentic experience with God.

Level You: The focus or spotlight is completely on the speaker. It's all about *you,* the person I am listening to. The skills of good listening are being utilized. The information is being received clearly. The listener is engaged with the speaker and the facts of the story, figuratively alongside the person, empathizing with what they are saying. The listener is noticing nonverbal cues, identifying emotions and picking up on the values of the other person. Listening at the You level allows the speaker to feel heard. This level of listening is what most small groups are striving for. People's needs are being met and they feel known because they have been heard. Level You

TO THE LIGHTHOUSE

"Now all the candles were lit up, and the faces on both sides of the table were brought nearer by the candlelight, and composed, as they had not been in the twilight, into a party round a table, for the night was now shut off by panes of glass, which, far from giving any accurate view of the outside world, rippled it so strangely that here, inside the room, seemed to be order and dry land; there, outside, a reflection in which things wavered and vanished, waterily. . . .

Some change went through them all, as if this had really happened, and they were all conscious of making a party together in a hollow, on an island; had their common cause against that fluidity out there. . . . Nothing need be said; nothing could be said. There it was, all round them. It partook . . . of eternity. . . . Of such moments, she thought, the thing is made that endures." (*Virginia Woolf,* To the Lighthouse) listening is what most people equate with good listening; you've probably read about it in a communications class, relationship book or leadership book.

Remember the 1997 movie *As Good as It Gets*? There is a brilliant illustration of Level Me and Level You listening in the scene called "Sad Stories." The three main characters, Carol (Helen Hunt), Melvin (Jack Nicholas) and Simon (Greg Kinnear), are in a car driving to see Simon's parents, whom he has been estranged from for some time. Carol asks him to share more about what caused their relationship to be damaged for so long. As soon as he starts, Carol realizes this is a conversation that requires her full attention and she pulls the car over to the side of the road. He starts sharing some terribly difficult things about his childhood. Melvin, who is in the back seat, feels threatened by the attention Simon is getting and tries repeatedly to steal the spotlight from Simon. He illustrates an exaggerated (and humorous) form of Level Me listening. All of his responses are about himself—*his* painful childhood, *his* father issues: "My father didn't come out of his room for eleven years!" Carol, on the other hand, is listening at Level You, practically perfectly. She is making eye contact, urging him to share more, asking questions and ignoring Melvin's interruptions. "Go ahead Simon. Please." The scene creates a great juxtaposition of Me and You listening.

Level Us: The third level involves and transcends the first two levels. It encompasses more than the people and the facts—it involves an awareness of the underlying dynamics: the actions and reactions, the general vibe, the presence of the Holy Spirit, the space or undercurrent in the room. All of that together helps the listener connect to the whole experience of the conversation—what's being said, and what's being revealed even though it's not verbalized. The listener engages with those intangibles and speaks into them. Rather than focusing the spotlight on one person in the group, it illuminates something more global that's happening in all of us, in the combination of us—everything that can be seen, felt, heard, tasted and smelled in the room.

TARA

ONE NIGHT MY HUSBAND AND I had asked another couple, Chad and Cora, to facilitate our small group. They had agreed to take part of the group when it was big enough to branch off and become facilitators, so we wanted to get people used to having them guide the group time as well. Chad and Cora came in that night with snow in their hair, holding freshly baked French bread, a bottle of wine and candles. A departure from our usual group routine, the evening was intended to be an experiential partaking of communion. Everything felt different that night. The lights were dimmed. Faces glowed. Exterior traffic noises seemed muffled. The scent of the candles filled the air. There was an element of the holy and the sacred that night.

○   ○   ○

Level Us listening is notoriously difficult to explain. It's listening holistically, listening for the overall vibe—like the kind of atmosphere created in Tara's group the night they took communion. Level Us is not the creation of any one person but is created in the intersection of everyone involved. It's the whole that is greater than the sum of its parts. One of the main differences between Level You and Level Us is that in Level Us the unspoken is addressed—it's identified and made part of the conversation.

Let's try taking an example of an ordinary conversation that moves between all three levels: Me, You and Us. Since Jenn is a newlywed, we'll pick on her and relate a conversation she had in the car with her husband Sammy over the course of a few hours one day.

Jenn: Rather than cycling one of the canyons today, do you want to ride our bikes to Todd and Jodi's house, hang out by the pool and then ride home?

Sammy: Are you saying you want to change our plans and do that? [Response suggests Level Me listening.]

Table 2.1. Three Levels of Communication

	Level Me	Level You	Level Us
Focus of listener	Self	Speaker	Speaker *and* experience
Typical listener responses	How what was said affects self A time when listener experienced something similar	Responding to the words being spoken Asking questions, offering information, advice or empathy	Responding simultaneously to the words being spoken *and* the unspoken elements present in the conversation
What happens to the spotlight that was on the speaker?	Moves to the listener	Stays on the speaker	Fills the space
Most suitable for	Doctor's appointments Counseling or coaching sessions where the listener is the client Receiving advice from others Interviews (when being asked questions about self)	Casual conversations Lectures, classroom learning experiences	Meaningful conversations on important matters such as spirituality, emotions, or major life decisions Small groups

Jenn [a bit sarcastically]: Well, yes, I wouldn't have suggested it if I didn't want to do it. We stayed home last night—it would be fun to have some time with friends. [Response suggests Level Me listening.]

[*Brief* period of silence. Sammy starts scanning radio stations.]

Jenn: It seems like this isn't what you had in mind for the day. That's okay. It was just a suggestion. It's a nice day and some time by the pool would be fun, but I know that's not what we had planned. Let's stick with our plan. We will see Todd and Jodi tomorrow. [Response suggests Level Us listening because she responded to the unspoken emotion and the vibe she was getting from Sammy.]

[*Later.* After cycling a canyon and stopping at the grocery store, where they ran into their friend Michelle.]

Sammy: You've been quiet ever since we ran into Michelle. What's up? [Response suggests Level Us listening because he is responding to the unspoken and the silence.]

Jenn: You're right. I'm thinking about how I've been home a lot lately. Talking with Michelle I realized I wish we'd made some plans for today or tonight. That's why I wanted to change our plans earlier. You get a lot of interaction with people at work that I don't get working at home. As much as I like being with you, I desire more time with others.

Sammy: That makes sense. Let's get out of the house tonight. [Response suggests Level You listening because he responded to the facts that were spoken.]

See the dance that takes place in conversations? How so much of what's really important and worth pursuing is in levels You and Us? This conversation is a simple example, but imagine if the topic had been, say, sex or finances.

Remember what David Whyte said? "A courageous conversation is the one you should be having." In courageous conversations, the unspoken is usually what's most essential to pursue—the vibe in the room, an internal gut response to a comment. And whether we're in the role of small group facilitator, spouse, friend, employer, parent or pastor, taking risks to follow our intuition may lead us toward the Spirit of God, toward the deeper truths of a conversation, toward the powerful and bold places that result in insight, inspiration, healing and growth. We need to be willing to trust our instincts and say things that risk being wrong. Sometimes we're just not sure, and we throw something out there to see if it connects. When that's done in a spirit of humility ("I could be wrong, but . . ."), our words spring not from a desire to be insightful, but from a desire to engage, even if that means looking a bit foolish sometimes.

MORE ON LEVEL US

Given that levels Me and You are much easier to understand and spot, we'll spend some additional time on Level Us. Us-level listening is the hardest not only to describe but also to practice. Let's look at two different aspects of it: the heart and undercurrents.

The heart. In Level Us the listener can name the emotions of the other person, hear the slight crack in the speaker's voice or see the joy in the other's eyes—if even just for a split second.

Sometimes we can see examples in Scripture of people engaging with each other at deep levels and picking up on the subtleties. Consider the passage from Nehemiah 2:

> In the month of Nisan in the twentieth year of King Artaxerxes, when wine was brought for him, I took the wine and gave it to the king. I had not been sad in his presence before, so the king asked me, "Why does your face look so sad when you are not ill? *This can be nothing but sadness of heart.*"
>
> I was very much afraid, but I said to the king, "May the king live forever! Why should my face not look sad when the city where my ancestors are buried lies in ruins, and its gates have been destroyed by fire?"
>
> The king said to me, "What is it you want?"
>
> Then I prayed to the God of heaven, and I answered the king, "If it pleases the king and if your servant has found favor in his sight, let him send me to the city in Judah where my ancestors are buried so that I can rebuild it."
>
> Then the king, with the queen sitting beside him, asked me, "How long will your journey take, and when will you get back?" It pleased the king to send me; so I set a time. (vv. 1-6, italics added)

King Artaxerxes inquires about Nehemiah's sadness. First he notices, then he takes the risk of inquiring about the unspoken. Even for a king, that was a risk. He might have heard something he didn't want to hear. He might have been told a lie. He might have received a lengthier response than he wanted. But what happened? Artaxerxes got a response that required something of him and cost him something. Because of that question, Nehemiah left the king's service, taking supplies and an army.

Given the risk involved in listening to someone's heart, we typically stay in our heads, dealing with logic and facts and reason. Are we curious about what we're missing? Or are others' emotions kind of scary to us? Perhaps our own emotions are sometimes scary to us. We'll need to be honest with ourselves about that, because getting to people's hearts and their emotions is what will make our discussions courageous. We need to be willing to go there first.

Emotions, our own or others', can be frightening. But we miss so much when we ignore them. Next time we notice a tear in someone's eye, we can simply say, "Tell me about the tear," and notice what happens. This simple question can be powerful. Recently, a small group prayer ended rather abruptly, and a group member who thought she would have more time to make her eyes presentable postprayer was suddenly face-to-face with the rest of the group while crying. Although in many group settings this demonstration of emotion would have been politely ignored, the facilitator decided to acknowledge the tears and asked about them. That simple question led to the group hearing some of the fears and self-doubt of the woman. It led to meaningful conversation about the truth of God's character, strength and love.

Undercurrents. Often the undercurrent is called "vibe." It's the space, the feeling in the room, encompassing both the energy and the physical environment. Us listening requires an awareness of this space. Although the listener is aware of what is being said (Level You), he or she is also acutely aware of what is going on in the space. The car engine turning over outside, the warmth of sunlight coming through a window, the loud music coming from the apartment upstairs—all of these things influence and contribute to what is being said.

A small group met in a park one afternoon to talk and pray about their lives. One participant, Stephen, was sharing how ever since he started his new job he was plagued with a sense that it wasn't a good fit for him and would not work out. He was deeply disappointed because it had taken him literally years to find this job, and when he finally landed it he thought it would be perfect. The group was trying to process with him, but kept getting interrupted by a very loud lawnmower going by. One member suggested moving to another place in the park, but they decided to wait and see if the noise would go away. After all, it was a beautiful view and they had a rare table in the shade.

The lawnmower noise became part of their Level Us, and after several more interruptions, eventually faded away as the mowing in their section was finished. A few minutes later, one person who had attended a leadership training we held on listening asked, "So, tell us Stephen, how is the lawnmower noise a metaphor for your circumstances?" This question generated some laughs, but Stephen decided he had nothing to lose by going there and responded, "Well, at first the noise was annoying and distracting. But I agreed with the others who thought it would go away, so I didn't think we needed to move. It took longer than I expected, but eventually the noise faded and then went away completely."

Another person followed up, "How might you apply that to your work situation?" After considering a bit longer he saw that the doubts he had were a lot like the noise of the lawnmower. They kept interrupting and distracting him. But, as with the proximity to the lawnmower at the park, Stephen had choices. He could wait and see or walk away and never know if the "noise" would have gone away and left him in a favorable situation.

Level Us is where a listener is most likely to engage with the whole truth about what is being spoken. In this way, Jesus listened to the Pharisees, listening beneath the surface of their spoken questions to address the real issues lurking in their hearts. If Jesus had answered their questions directly, he would have missed the point. When we ignore or miss what's going on at Level Us, we miss the depth behind the words being spoken, like James and John missed it when they responded to Jesus' announcement of his death by requesting the best seats in the house (classic Level Me listening).

Most of us know that listening is not supposed to be "all about me," even if we sometimes slip into Level Me listening. But it's also true that listening is not "all about you." Instead, Level Us listening moves us into engagement with God and what he is doing. What does God want to reveal? Where is he at work? That's the most important thing, above my agenda or your agenda. Engagement with God is where real insight into the other is gained. That's where powerful things become possible and where healing takes place.

READING SCRIPTURE AT LEVEL US

Level Us listening applies to reading Scripture too. Sometimes we forget that reading the Bible is an interactive process, but it is. It is a dialogue, not a monologue. Level Us listening in Scripture reading takes place in the heart of the reader. All of us bring our senses, experiences and intuitions to the text. We are given the words on the page, representing actions and thoughts and ideas. But only as we engage with Scripture does it come to life for us, its meaning seeping to deeper levels in us. Look at this passage from 1 Samuel 1:4-8:

> Whenever the day came for Elkanah to sacrifice, he would give portions of the meat to his wife Peninnah and to all her sons and daughters. But to Hannah he gave a double portion because he loved her, and the LORD had closed her womb. Because the LORD had closed Hannah's womb, her rival kept provoking her in order to irritate her. This went on year after year. Whenever Hannah went up to the house of the LORD, her rival provoked her till she wept and would not eat. Her husband Elkanah would say to her, "Hannah, why are you weeping? Why don't you eat? Why are you downhearted? Don't I mean more to you than ten sons?"

Imagine the dynamics of living in Elkanah's household. Two wives, one the favorite. What was going on in Elkanah's heart? He likely was trying to make up for Hannah's barrenness with the double portion. Well-intentioned maybe, but not recognizing that by so obviously demonstrating his partiality he was likely making things even harder for Hannah. In the meantime the other wife was bearing children at a time when offspring were highly valued, yet she not receiving the honor or love she likely felt was due her. What was going on in Peninnah's heart? Jealousy, anger, a desire for recognition? And Hannah, so distraught by the taunting, was unable to eat. Unable to escape from her rival, desperately wanting a child, Hannah likely felt that her options were running out. How would she continue to live in such a hostile environment? And then Elkanah, apparently clueless, asked, "Don't I mean more to you than ten sons?" and missed the point entirely.

Obviously, with such interpretations, we may be wrong sometimes. Maybe Peninnah didn't feel a desire for recognition. And maybe Elkanah's comment at the end was helpful rather than off-target. But by imagining, we have engaged with the text at a much deeper level than if we had simply read for information or read it on a Me level: "So what is God saying to *me* in this passage?" Scripture, although certainly having applications for our lives, is not ultimately about me. There is a larger story to engage and enter into. Learning to engage Scripture at Level Us leads to more powerful interactions in our groups. We experience sacred moments that lead us further toward God.

What is the larger story about Hannah? Why is this story important to us? Why is it important to God? What is he communicating to us about himself? That he wants us to consider how we respond to not getting what we want? That he wants us to know he loves us even when we're not getting what we want? That polygamy is complicated? There are a lot of possible ways to engage with the text and God. And that's what reading Scripture at Level Us leads to.

STUCK IN A ME MOMENT

Me listening presents such a formidable barrier to such engagement. It's hard to get out of Me moments. We can get stuck there, and sometimes not just for a moment. Sometimes it takes weeks or months. And that is okay once in a while, especially in times of crisis and healing. But it's never the final destination. As we facilitate groups, we can get stuck in the Me level in some specific ways.

JENN

I QUIT SMOKING WHEN I WAS TWENTY-TWO YEARS OLD. I remember how great it felt to overcome this addiction—I'd started smoking at a very young age and had been smoking for many years when I quit. I was quite proud when I accomplished this feat—perhaps a little too proud.

Everyone I knew or met shortly after quitting was labeled as either a smoker or nonsmoker. And people who smoked were now also labeled weak and unhealthy. This was the lens I saw everything through because it was such a significant event for me.

Seeing things (of God) through our own lens. When we get stuck seeing things through our own lens—whatever has happened to us recently, whatever God has shown us recently, whatever has been meaningful to us recently—this becomes the prescription for everyone else too. If therapy has been helpful for me, I'll recommend it for you too. If a spiritual retreat spoke to me, whenever someone has a problem, whatever it may be, I'll recommend that they take a spiritual retreat. That will fix it. And that's the point, right? Fixing other people's problems?

Remember our friend Simone? The one who listened to the Spirit, noticed the emotions of another woman in the group, and asked about her father? Simone learned a few lessons about trying to fix others' problems the hard way. Simone walked away from her small group that evening with a strong sense that Ashley's negative feelings toward her father because he did not provide financially were causing her to idealize men who were the opposite—highly successful with careers that came first. At the time, Ashley was dating a man who fit that profile and the relationship was becoming quite messy. This man did not have most of the other important qualities Ashley said she wanted—a solid spiritual foundation, common hobbies and interests. He often cancelled their dates because he was working late, and he didn't do much to show that he valued her. He was all about work. Simone felt that what was revealed to her was common sense: until Ashley dealt with the disappointments from her father she would always gravitate toward these unhealthy relationships. So next time Simone saw Ashley, she told her that. No prelude, no building up to that point. Just said it. Ashley was understandably hurt. She felt judged, like Simone didn't understand her and didn't understand her relationship. From a point of deep connection the week before, forged through asking questions and listening, trust was now damaged.

Was Simone right about Ashley's father and boyfriend issues? Maybe. Possibly through conversation and friendship and prayer, Ashley would have come to some of those realizations on her own. But that isn't the point. The point—especially in small groups—is not to fix others or give them the right answers. Particularly if they're not even asking the questions. Simone's dispatching of Ashley's relationship problems in a sentence or two was not only unhelpful but damaging. Again, not a new concept but an old one: "Everyone should be quick to listen, slow to speak" (James 1:19).

The beauty of a small group lies in the way it challenges our perceptions, when someone else makes a comment and we think to ourselves, *How could they possibly think that?* The route to growth lies in putting on the other person's shoes for a time and walking around. Maybe there are good reasons they think that way. By trying on each other's shoes, we can help each other see God for who he really is. And we know him better.

This experience is particularly powerful in groups that are multiethnic, international or multigenerational. Sometimes the way we experience God in the United States is much different than it is in Europe, Africa or Asia. The differences are striking, even among believers, and we have much to learn from people who are different.

Groups can also help us see some of the religious baggage we're carrying.

FROM AN EARLY AGE, I'VE SEEN GOD AS MORE TRANSCENDENT than immanent. His primary characteristics are holiness and justice. The Old Testament has always made perfect sense to me—if you step out of line, God will strike you down. He is a stern judge, and there's no margin for error. Maybe some of you share that perception. But most of you are thinking, "Really? That's a bizarre view of God. Wonder where she got that—maybe she hasn't gotten to the Gospels yet in her Bible reading." Different perspectives like that help me develop a more balanced and accurate view of God.

○ ○ ○

Lack of listening-skills development. Another way we get stuck in the Me level has to do with listening. Sometimes we are not good listeners simply due to lack of information—listening doesn't come naturally to most of us, so if we haven't been intentional about learning how to listen, we likely aren't doing it very well. Or maybe it's a lack of practice. Listening well requires a great deal of self-discipline, so practicing in short spurts is best at first. And when attempting to listen to God, try different methods, places or postures. There's no one right way. It's a risk, because sometimes we won't hear anything. But when we do suspect we are hearing something, we need to act on it. We need to take the risk of looking foolish by stepping out on a limb and engaging even when we aren't certain. Good listening is required for intimacy, whether that intimacy is with God or others.

DO THIS

Spend an evening discussing the topic of listening with your group. Ask everyone to share when they felt the group was really listening to them versus a time when they felt unheard. Ask for their thoughts and ideas on how to improve the collective listening of the group.

Performance orientation. When we find ourselves afraid of appearing weak, stupid, vulnerable, naive, uninformed, overinformed, prideful, condescending and so on, that's when we know we're stuck in a Me moment. It's all about me—how I'm being perceived, what people are thinking about me, whether or not they're impressed, whether or not they like me. Odds are they're not thinking nearly as much about me as I am. Here's another tell-tale sign: *I'll just nod my head a lot to show I'm listening.* When we catch ourselves thinking that, we're caught in a Me moment. Now, not that there's anything wrong with head-nodding. It's just that when it's stemming from a desire to protect our own image, it can't also be stemming from authenticity and trust. Maybe too much of my self-worth is coming from being the Bible Answer Man or the Compassionate Pastoral Woman. That's an "ouch" kind of thing to look at. But it may be the only path out of a Me moment.

Emotions and judgment getting in the way. Remember the "Knowing Yourself" chapter at the beginning of the book? The ways in which we are unaware of ourselves can trip us up in significant ways when it comes to listening. What irks you? What's going to suck you into a debate or cause you to dismiss someone's comments or opinion? Look out for what hits your emotion button or judgment button:

- *Emotions:* Is she really asking for prayer about her body image? She probably weighs thirty pounds less than I do. The nerve!

- *Judging:* I cannot believe he's telling me he struggles with homosexual thoughts. That's really awful. How could he claim to be a *Christian* and say this?

Not asking questions. Although there's another chapter on asking questions, it bears mention here because not asking questions is one of the surest signs of a Me moment. When we're not curious about people, they feel it. According to studies, most people (especially women) provide a bit of information and then evaluate the level of interest in the listener. If the listener asks questions, the speaker will offer more of the story, more of themselves. Questions play a key role in listening, as they bring forth additional material, not to mention help people feel cared for and respected.

If you're feeling bad just about now, know that it's not unusual to experience most of the issues we've addressed while leading a small group discussion. We all wonder what people think of us sometimes, and we all think judgmental thoughts sometimes. But the more self-awareness we develop, the more we'll be able to self-manage and keep the focus on God instead of on ourselves. And from that vantage point, we may hear God desiring to use our lens or our emotions to do something powerful in the group. The rules of engagement are unpredictable and far from formulaic. Just when we think we know what we're doing, God does something new.

As the river rushes along we can be listening, paying attention to the bubbling on the surface, but also paying attention to what might be happening beneath the surface. Sometimes in those still places, the places where it doesn't seem like much is going on, we are right where we need to be. And sometimes, if we are listening, we can hear the voice of God in those silences.

EXERCISES AND REFLECTION QUESTIONS

Exercise
Read Ruth 1:3-16. What's present at Level Us?

Reflection Questions

1. What courageous conversations have you had with yourself, in your own heart and mind, and with your spouse, children or other loved ones? What courageous conversations have you had with your small group? What courageous conversations are you sensing you might need to have?

2. During your small group meeting this week, pay attention to how often you are in levels Me, You and Us. What do you notice? What are the things that distract you from Level Us? What is one new habit or practice that you can integrate into your meetings that will increase the likelihood of Level Us listening?

3. What causes you to get stuck in Me moments? What might God be trying to reveal to you?

4. What are you discerning about someone in your small group? How will you serve this person?

5. What risk might God be asking you to take with your small group?

6. When have you thought you "heard God wrong"? What other perspectives might you have about those circumstances?

7. To what degree do you believe that God is good? What impact does

this perception have on your small group?

8. In what areas of your life has God been silent? How have you wrestled with that? How have you felt? In what ways can you engage with him in the silence?

9. What is the Us Level as you're reading this right now? Even if you're alone, take a moment to identify your emotions and the environment around you. Where and how do you sense God at work?

4

STIRRING
THE WATERS

Asking Good Questions

What do you want me to do for you?

MATTHEW 20:32

When facilitators don't know the answer to a question, they are generally instructed to own up, admit that they don't know and offer to find out. Then they research (usually by calling the pastor) and come back next week with the answer. Right? Except that it misses the point of small groups. They are not about answers. They are more about interactive experiences.

Small groups are not so much about the answers as they are about the questions. The facilitator should be asking far more questions than answering them. Questions form the skeleton outline of a group—the basic structure on which everything else hangs.

TARA

IF I WERE GOING TO FACILITATE A GROUP but had only one skill, I'd pick this one: the ability to ask good questions. It doesn't matter what kind of group it is—it could be anything from an in-depth Bible study to a support group. I'd still pick asking good questions. When I was a small groups pastor, so many potential facilitators I talked with had the same fear about leading a group: "I don't know enough—I've never been to seminary. What if they ask questions and I don't know the answers?" What they don't realize is that 90 percent of leading a group is about having the right questions, not having the right answers.

○   ○   ○

Questions are the banks of the river, providing some definition and direction as the current carries things along. Too much limitation and the flow of the river is impeded. Too little and the river becomes directionless, spreading the water out into a broad, stagnant marsh.

Questions—not statements—form a general outline for group discussion. If facilitators walk in with a list of questions, they don't necessarily have to use them all; they may change the order and other questions may come to mind in the moment. But by preparing some good questions ahead of time, a facilitator can mine the insights of the group and help people engage the topic at hand.

Questions are better than statements as the foundation for a group because they are interactive, they go somewhere, they make us engage. Most people don't grow closer to God through information. That's a modernist idea. The era of modernism passed down to us the idea

DO THIS

Prepare a list of questions for each small group gathering. People remember better what they discover for themselves by answering questions. And questions lead to discussions that create an experience, an event that is memorable.

that knowledge will save us—if we know enough about the world, we can tame it. This idea has enjoyed a good deal of popularity throughout the last few centuries but is far from universal.

Is there a place for information? For knowledge? For learning some basic information about the Christian faith? Absolutely. Sometimes people simply need information. Sometimes it is helpful to suggest to a new believer, "Start by reading the Gospel of John and then let's meet and we'll go over it." Information and suggestions and content are helpful. The problem is that we tend to go there *first*. The *first* place to go is to engage with the person as a person—and that's often best done by asking him or her a question or two.

DO THIS

Ask your group, "What would you do differently in your life if you were 100 percent convinced that God is good?" What does being good mean? What do you notice about what people in your group believe about God? Pick three stories from the Bible that might challenge their beliefs.

Sometimes when someone in a small group asks an informational question, they're looking for more than just information. As a facilitator, look beneath the surface. Informational questions can be a safer way of broaching subjects that may not feel safe. So by all means, dispense information when necessary. Just don't *start* there.

Say someone in a group asks about the apparent difference between the God of the Old Testament and the God of the New Testament. That's a legitimate question, but if the facilitator immediately goes into an explanation of dispensationalism or covenant theology, he or she is likely to have missed the real point of the question.

Usually there's an underlying question more along the lines of, What is God like? Will he strike me down if I anger him? Or is he my buddy? Or something else? Am I supposed to fear God or love God? Does he care about me? Does justice matter to him? How do other people experience God? So, for instance, that last question might present a better direction to go. When someone asks about the difference between the God of the Old Testament and the God of the New, the facilitator could respond by asking, "How do you experience God?" directing it to not just the person who asked the question, but the whole group—and the discussion moves to a deeper and likely more productive level.

In the novel *Gilead* by Marilynne Robinson, Jack Boughton asks preacher John Ames, "So, reverend, I would like to hear your views on the doctrine of predestination." And it's not until some time later, after several decidedly unproductive conversations about predestination, that we find how troubled Jack is, haunted by the sins of his past and his lack of faith. Once you understand where he's coming from, his question about predestination has a decidedly personal flavor. Jack feels an increasing sense of distress that religion has never meant anything to him, that even though his father was a preacher, his father's words never reached him. He feels as if grace is absent from his life. Why wouldn't God let him in on this? That's the real question he's asking. When we allow questions and answers to remain on an informational level, we risk missing the more significant questions beneath the surface.

People in the Bible had many different experiences of God; some experienced him as absent, angry and capricious. Our experience, whether an accurate reflection of God's character or not, matters. Once we've acknowledged our experience, then it's a matter of deciding what conclusions to draw. In small groups, we can find ways to validate people's perceptions while still juxtaposing those experiences with Scripture that will lead them to truths about God. The problems come when we just gloss over people's experiences and expect that confrontation with the truth of Scripture will have a meaningful effect on what they believe about God.

WRESTLING WITH GOD

As much as we may attempt to focus on asking good questions, people may pressure us to provide them with answers. Lizzie became a Christian in her mid-twenties and promptly discovered that she had some major adjustments to make in how she approached sex. Based on her newfound biblical knowledge, she decided that premarital sex was now out of the question for her, but she wanted answers about how far is too far. Lizzie took this question to her women's group, but walked away frustrated because they responded to her question with a question. Even as she got more persistent, they wouldn't answer her question but continued to ask, "How do you sense God is guiding you regarding sexual boundaries?" As Lizzie reflected on the experience years later, she said that even though she was frustrated at the time, she now thought that was one of the best questions she'd ever been asked in a small group because it required her to wrestle with God for an answer. She also wondered what kind of damage may have been done had the group given her a pat (and likely arbitrary) answer.

Although having a certain amount of information about God is necessary for faith in and action toward him, much of the real knowledge of God comes through wrestling, wondering, questioning, doubting, dialoguing, resisting, risking and sometimes making a fool of yourself. Small groups need to be safe places for people to go through that process: to ask the questions we are really wondering about, those that might put God in a bad light, those that we don't have the answers to.

TARA

ONE MORNING I WAS OUT TO BREAKFAST with some of the people in my small group. I was in the throes of a move and real estate deal. My husband and I were moving to a nicer house, but we also had a house to sell, and the deal felt touch-and-go, ready to collapse at any moment, so we were pretty stressed. We were talking about praying for the situation, and I asked (swallowing my conservative Bible college past), "Do you think God really cares about my house? I mean, there are plenty of people in the world who don't have houses at all, and I already have one that I'm trying to sell so I can get a nicer one. When I step back, it doesn't really seem like something God would be overly concerned with. Isn't praying about this actually selfish?"

People had various—and conflicting—thoughts on that, and I didn't come away with an answer. But I didn't really expect one, and to be honest, if someone had given me their "answer" it would have missed the point entirely. I would likely have come away feeling unheard and afraid people thought I was unspiritual. So I didn't find an answer, but I did feel like I came away having been honest about where I was before God and before others. People took my concerns seriously, without writing me off, dismissing me or condescending to give me what they considered the self-evident answer. I felt heard and understood. And I had some other perspectives to consider that I would not have thought of on my own. And that was what I needed to grow closer to God then and there.

○   ○   ○

A good small group is a safe place to ask the questions that are really on our minds. We all wonder about things that our interior censor tells us not to ask out loud. Someone might think we were unspiritual, a bad person or simply uninformed. What if they are condescending? What if they give us the easy answer, the one we already know but isn't strong enough to satisfy? What if they tell us "all things work together for good"? We need safe places to ask the hard questions. And we need safe places to test out those interior responses, answers of a sort, that we feel aren't always appropriate.

A SMALL GROUP I WAS A PART OF A FEW YEARS AGO—that, incidentally, was being led by Tara and her husband, Mark—was studying the Gospel of John. We were several chapters in and had read numerous stories about the Pharisees not getting it, being thick and mean-spirited, and then intentionally putting roadblocks in the way of Jesus. One man in our group who was exploring Christianity had had enough. Sean had been getting more and more frustrated with each of these encounters between Jesus and the religious leaders, and finally he blurted out, "I just want to take out a machine gun and mow all those Pharisees down!" Brief, stunned silence. Sean looked around at the frozen expressions, then made a much more tentative inquiry: "Should I not have said that?" But really, people were more surprised at the manner of expression than at the sentiment itself. Sean, brand new to the Scriptures, was engaging with them. He wasn't just studying them, he was experiencing them, reading them the way they were intended to be read: experientially and in community.

If we read the Scriptures and are unmoved by them, we aren't really engaging with them. Scripture itself models the engagement with God that comes through asking the hard questions, expressing the thoughts that may not be appropriate but are nonetheless real. Consider the Psalms. Sitting down and reading psalms for an hour will take you on an emotional roller coaster, to the depths and the heights and right back down again, sometimes all in the same psalm. They are raw and emotional, and written primarily by a man after God's own heart. A man who did not always do the right thing but was willing to dive into the deep end with God.

And David's questions were not always the polite religious ones. A quick survey of the Psalms will reveal many passages like this one:

> Will the Lord reject forever?
>   Will he never show his favor again?
> Has his unfailing love vanished forever?
>   Has his promise failed for all time?
> Has God forgotten to be merciful?
>   Has he in anger withheld his compassion? (Psalm 77:7-9)

Apparently David was not afraid of putting God in a bad light with his questions. He was not afraid of being too much for God. That—not feeling the need to "protect" God by sparing him the truly difficult questions—*that* is faith.

ASKING QUESTIONS OF SCRIPTURE

Here is the absolute simplest, most basic way to lead a small group discussion: Choose any passage of Scripture, and write out six or seven open-ended questions that could get people started talking about it. That's it. Really.

The goal is to create questions that will encourage people to open up to dialogue with each other around the passage. Here's a sample passage and some questions created directly from the text.

I rejoiced greatly in the Lord that at last you renewed your concern for me. Indeed, you were concerned, but you had no opportunity to show it. I am not saying this because I am in need, for I have learned to be content whatever the circumstances. I know what it is to be in need, and I know what it is to have plenty. I have learned the secret of being content in any and every situation, whether well fed or hungry, whether living in plenty or in want. I can do all this through him who gives me strength. (Philippians 4:10-13)

1. What tensions do you think Paul might have been feeling with this community?

2. When have you been in need and felt forgotten by your friends?

3. How content did you feel in those circumstances?

4. What do you suppose Paul means by the "secret of being content"? What would that look like in real life?

5. What do you believe this teaches about Paul's relationship to God?

6. What do these verses tell us about what God desires for his followers?

7. In what areas of life are you struggling with contentment?

8. In what areas do you feel what seems like a legitimate desire for more? How does that fit in with contentment?

9. What are some of the strengths of God that you desire in your life?

There. Now you're ready for a group discussion.

TRUSTING THE PROCESS

One of the most challenging things about leading a group this way is that we have to trust the people there to have something to say. We have to trust that they can hear from the Spirit for themselves. And we have to trust the process—that responding to questions in the context of community will lead to growth. It's a mysterious process, but the more we trust it, the more we can see it at work.

Honest questions move people toward a deeper, more examined faith. Powerful questions take people into their hearts, into their own souls—and that's where God can connect and speak to them.

ONE NIGHT IN A GROUP MEETING, I was sharing during the prayer-request time, asking for both prayer and accountability. My family was out of state and I wanted to try to stay better connected to them. I felt like the distance was making that more challenging, and it seemed that no matter how hard I tried, I couldn't make myself take the necessary steps to stay connected. Several people had suggestions: I could schedule calls, I could plan more trips back home, I could develop a weekly habit of doing something every Sunday night to stay connected. The advice seemed to be taking me nowhere, and I began to feel more and more discouraged.

Then the facilitator asked me a very simple question: "What do you want?" It was like a dam had burst. I could feel tears burning in the corners of my eyes, as I burst out, "I want them to *listen* to me. I want them to ask me how I am doing and I want them to want to know the *real* answer." Being asked this question—such a simple question—caused me to connect with my heart and got at the very core of the matter. This experience resulted in some powerful conversations and deeper intimacy with my family. With the initial suggestions, I'd stayed stuck in my head trying to apply logic and solutions, which got me nowhere without understanding what was going on at a deeper, more experiential level.

○   ○   ○

Although the example above is more on the personal side, the same is true of questions about the Bible. One group had begun debating the merits of Calvinism and Arminianism. After several weeks of discussion that seemed to be going nowhere, the facilitator asked, "How has this discussion affected your understanding of God's character?" People had a huge range of answers, all of which dealt with the mystery of God. Good questions can move Bible studies out of the realm of the theoretical and academic and into the heart of Scripture.

POWERFUL QUESTIONS

Often the simplest questions are the best. If you look at both of the questions above (What do you want? How has this discussion been affecting your faith?), you'll notice several things about them. They're both relatively simple. They're both open-ended, allowing for a wide range of responses. They both require some reflection and encourage insight and awareness. Take a look at the chart we've provided on the next page to check out some of the qualities of powerful questions, and some of the qualities that rob questions of their power.

DO THIS

Come up with a list of your top ten most powerful small group questions. Keep them on hand for times when you're having a hard time keeping the conversation flowing. Examples: What are some of the doubts you have about what we're talking about? When have you experienced something like this [what you are discussing] in your life? What else have you learned about this topic?

There's a board game from the 1980s called *Bible Trivia*. It's packed with closed-ended questions that have clear right-or-wrong answers. Question: What did Jacob give to Joseph to show he was his favorite son? Answer: a coat of many colors. Question: What animal did the Israelites make an idol of and worship while Moses was on the mountain getting the 10 commandments? Answer: a calf.

But what makes a good trivia game for children makes a less-than-satisfactory small group experience for adults. Closed questions are questions that have either a yes/no answer or only one right answer. They are usually informational. When closed questions are asked in small groups, most adults either feel fearful (What if I get it wrong? How embarrassing!) or patronized (Do they think I am stupid? I finished doing fill-in-the-blank worksheets in fourth grade!).

One of the simplest ways to improve the quality of questions asked in groups is to make sure they're all open-ended. Start by surveying all the questions just before group, and before long it will become a habit to formulate them as open-ended.

Powerful questions . . .	*Powerful questions are not . . .*
• take people deep into their heart—to the core of the matter (What are you making more important than your relationship with God?)	• leading (Do you really think that's what Paul is saying?)
• result in change/growth (What aspect of this discussion will you apply to your life?)	• manipulative (Don't you think that's judgmental?)
• are simple and direct (What's in your way?)	• "why" questions (Why would you doubt that?)
• build self-awareness (What do you gain or lose by holding that viewpoint?)	• usually limited to the intellectual arena (although some good questions can be, if they are then followed up with questions that move the discussion deeper)
• aren't easy to answer (How do you diminish God's majesty?)	• closed (Was Sarah lacking faith?)
• stir emotion (What are you having trouble admitting?)	
• instill self-confidence (What do you know is true in this situation?)	
• send people looking for an answer or direction (How do you want this to affect your life?)	
• invite introspection (How does your belief differ from your actions?)	
• cause people to stop and think (How does this challenge your faith?)	
• lead to deeper creativity and insight (What are some perspectives you could explore on this?)	
• challenge people's thinking (What are your assumptions?)	
• help solve problems (What are some possible directions?)	

Usually closed questions can be readily transformed into open-ended questions. Take an earlier example: Do you think Sarah was lacking faith? It could be rephrased in several different ways: (1) Comment on Sarah's faith. (2) How do you think Sarah was feeling at that point? (3) Describe Sarah's trust in God at this point. (4) How do you see Sarah relating to God here?

Whereas the closed question yields only a yes or a no (one of which is almost certainly not the response the facilitator was looking for), the latter options allow people to engage with the text, use their imaginations, put themselves in Sarah's shoes, and provide differing perspectives without fear of judgment.

DO THIS

Many people are more apt to be in their head with thoughts rather than in their heart with feelings. Dare to ask the questions that will take people into their emotions. If someone gives you a well-thought-out response to a question, ask them to answer the same question with their heart.

Often one of the signs of a good question is that the facilitator doesn't already know the answer. It's okay for the facilitator to ask a question, without knowing the answer, and observe what develops. But remember that sometimes the people in the group won't know the answer either. Good questions that require people to dig deeper are often met initially with silence. The facilitator has had a while to think about the question, but the rest of the group hasn't, and it may take them a while to respond. Learn to become comfortable with silence.

WADING INTO UNCHARTED WATERS

In short, open-ended questions require us to think for ourselves. And thinking for ourselves, especially in the context of community where others can challenge us and broaden our perspectives, is one of the surest ways to grow. It's also one of the scariest. What if we come to unapproved conclusions? What if the other group members kick us out for theological reasons? What if, what if . . . ? If the small group is like a river, moving with the current, questions are like little branches dipping in and shaking things up, or like children skipping stones: they stir the waters and require us to change direction (rethink). And there are few things scarier than changing direction when you're already in deep water.

Yet without that periodic rethinking, we become unaware, carried along passively by the current. We also miss the opportunities for growth and change that creative thought can bring. What if the job I felt was a gift from God is only for a season? What if I'm supposed to step out and start that business I've always kept in the corner of my mind? What if I'm supposed to step aside from a ministry that's going well and try some new way to use my gifts, some way that is untested and that might lead to failure?

Look broadly, and you'll see that several different movements and professions have been directing energy and research toward the power of questions. Consider therapists, counselors, life coaches, spiritual directors: all of these use intentional conversations borne of good questions to draw people out and help them reflect and grow.

The idea is that questions, along with the thought they generate, have inherent value. They are taking us somewhere. Through questions, we find healing, discovery, insight, new direction. And those are infinitely more powerful when the answers are pulled from within ourselves, where we can hear the Holy Spirit speaking.

AS A SMALL GROUPS PASTOR, I HAD A CONVERSATION with my supervisor, who has exceptional coaching skills, in which I related a situation I was trying to figure out how to handle. I'd had several conversations lately with a small group facilitator who was having some problems in his group, and after describing those exchanges along with many specifics, options and possible directions I could go, my supervisor asked me, "What do you think he needs right now?" With that one question, he got at the deeper issue. Aside from the specifics, aside from all the possible options at my disposal, what kind of support did that leader need at that time?

I RECENTLY STARTED ENGAGING IN SPIRITUAL DIRECTION—the art of intentional, focused conversations about life with God. During a meeting with my spiritual director, Tim, he said, "Since we're already on the topic of intimacy, tell me the members of the Trinity with whom you have the greatest and least intimacy." Simple enough. It was my answer this time—not the question—that stopped me in my tracks. Did I really have the most intimacy with the Holy Spirit and the least with Jesus? And isn't that unusual? Being asked this simple question sent me searching deep within my heart for answers. Was there something unsafe about Jesus to me? Why was I keeping an unintentional distance from him? And how was that affecting my spiritual formation? My ability to love others? Tim then asked me to come up with a question to ponder that week that I thought might lead me to deeper understanding. The question I formulated had to do with patterns in my relationships with men.

Within the few hours that followed our meeting, it became apparent I had not formulated the best question. I found that a better question centered on what things I was making up about Jesus. Pondering *that* question is what led to real insight. Tim later shared with me that he suspected it would be more powerful for me to consider my relationship with Jesus, but he decided to wait and see where my question led. The experience was far more meaningful to me than if Tim had told me his hunch because the clarity came directly from the Spirit of God.

○   ○   ○

Asking questions rests on the assumption that people are able to hear God speak for themselves, that the Holy Spirit is at work within them. Giving answers rests on the assumption that others will not be able to figure it out on their own—they need our help. We hear from God on their behalf and then tell them what they are to do or believe or think. Yet when we are told what to do, we seldom have the ownership or investment or passion that will carry us along the course of action. But if someone has a vision or belief that they have heard from God themselves, even the most challenging obstacles will be met with energy and creativity. Often when we are afraid to ask questions, it is because we do not trust others or their process.

JENN

I HAD AN OPPORTUNITY TO SPEAK AT A CONFERENCE held at my church for people who "might be married someday" (because *singles conference* is one of those terms we don't use anymore). Given that I didn't get married until I was thirty-seven years old, I had some credibility on the subject of waiting for the right one. I shared a story about one of my low points as a single to illustrate a point about getting legitimate needs met illegitimately.

I was a bridesmaid (again!) during a time when I was struggling with being single. In an attempt to make myself feel better, I was enjoying the attention I was getting from what I initially saw as innocent flirting with a couple of men at the wedding. But something came over me that changed my heart. I realized my behavior was actually inappropriate, which made me feel even worse about myself.

Shortly after realizing this, I was approached by another bridesmaid who I'd just met that weekend. She said, "Jenn, this may seem strange, but I feel like God is asking me to tell you that he has not forgotten about you." Even telling the story a few years later at this conference caused my eyes to fill with tears. And I was surprised by the number of tear-filled eyes in the audience staring back at me. I wish I'd stopped at that moment and said, "What would you do differently if you truly believed God has not forgotten about you?" rather than continuing to tell them what I did differently. I wish I'd taken a little less control of their learning.

Sometimes groups can get pretty comfortable letting the facilitator do all of the work. Someone in the group will say something controversial or vulnerable or even just totally off-base, and all eyes will land on the facilitator. *How's he or she going to handle this one?* One of our friends told us his favorite question—especially in circumstances like these—is simply, "What questions does the group have about that?" This question puts the responsibility for engagement and responses back in the lap of the group. It also communicates that the group leader is not the authority figure handing down verdicts, and that communication doesn't run from group member to facilitator, back to group leader, back to facilitator, like a tennis match. Instead, it's more like a web, with communication moving in multiple directions.

DO THIS

To improve the quality of the questions your group asks one another, devote a portion of an evening to getting curious and practicing forming powerful questions. Have someone share a story about something going on in his or her life. Then have the others ask that person questions (without anyone answering the questions) until all questions are exhausted. At the end, have the storyteller share which questions were most powerful and why. Ask if there was a question that wasn't asked which would have been even more powerful. If time allows, repeat with two or three other people in the group.

Sometimes facilitators are afraid that a question like "How does the group want to respond to that?" will communicate that we do not know how to respond. And maybe we don't. That's okay. Maybe someone else does. After all, the Holy Spirit is at work in all of us. And sometimes when we don't know what to say, God is speaking to someone else. But even when we do have an idea about what to say, reflecting the responsibility back to the group can make some powerful statements: They can share how God is speaking to them in the moment. They have something valuable to offer. They are responsible to engage with one another. Their thoughts and questions make a difference.

JESUS IS THE ANSWER

We've presented many good reasons for facilitators to focus on asking good questions. Yet with small groups, and with church in general, we have historically given short-shrift to questions. Questions are associated with doubt, the antithesis of faith. We in the church are in the business of giving answers. We are to be skilled at apologetics; we've been instructed to "always be prepared to give an answer to everyone who asks you to give the reason for the hope that you have" (1 Peter 3:15). And haven't we all been told at least once that Jesus is the answer? (What the question was, we are not sure. Generally, it doesn't seem to matter.)

DO THIS

For each Bible-related or content-related question you ask that targets understanding, ask at least one question that relates the content or the passage to real-life situations or needs.

Sometimes giving a premature answer can short-circuit someone's necessary thought process. Even a really good answer, if given by someone else, will have far less power than if it is pulled from within the person asking the question. And more importantly, it seems there are times God wants us to wrestle with him, just like Jacob did. And there's no shortcut for that. The process is part of the growth. We're back to wrestling with God here, using questions as a route to growth.

A friend who is in a small group that is focused on spiritual direction shared recently that even though the group's purpose is focused on asking questions, they still have the natural propensity to provide answers. The individuals had just completed an exercise on scriptural meditation and came back together to debrief. One of the members expressed that he had struggled with one of the verses in the passage. "I don't understand what that's supposed to mean. It doesn't seem consistent with how I see the character of God." Another member of the group began explaining the passage, giving several possible interpretations of the verse in question. The facilitator gently intervened, explaining that the focus of spiritual direction is not to provide answers but to provide companionship along the road as people explore.

Having answers is obviously part of our journey, as is knowing what we believe. Yet, when we look at the Gospels, we find that Jesus gave very few answers and used questions an awful lot. "What do you want me to do for you?" (Matthew 20:32). "Do you want to get well?" (John 5:6). "How are you going to believe what I say?" (John 5:47). "What are you discussing together as you walk along?" (Luke 24:17). "What do you think?" (Matthew 21:28). " 'But what about you?' he asked, 'Who do you say I am?' " (Matthew 16:15).

According to Richard Rohr, Jesus asked 183 questions of various individuals and groups in the Gospels. And often when people asked him questions, instead of answering them, he responded in a way designed to make them think, often asking a question in turn. Actually, of all those questions, Jesus answered only three.

Now, we should clarify that we don't think it's always bad to give an answer when someone asks a question. Sometimes answers can be good and helpful. Often with new followers of Christ or people needing some content and grounding in what the Bible is about, answers are just what's needed.

In other cases, clarification requires an answer. Just a few weeks ago in one of our small groups, people were talking about areas of sin or struggle in their lives. One man was sharing about Internet poker. And another man, new to the faith, asked, "Sorry to back up the discussion, but what is it about Internet poker that's a sin? I don't understand." Far from backing things up, the discussion was enhanced by further clarification of motivation and a discussion of the distinctions between gambling as an occasional pastime and gambling out of idolatry or addiction.

But often we focus on answers because the questions scare us. And there's a reason for that. Questions can make us appear unintelligent. Questions lead us down unapproved paths. Questions force us to discover (and possibly explore) what's happening on a deeper level. Do we *really* want to know what's going on in our own heart? It might not be good, and what if we can't fix it on our own? Or do we really want to know what's going on in someone else's heart? After all, that may result in responsibility—we might have to get more involved in his or her life—and don't most of us have enough to worry about already? There is a risk inherent in asking good questions and really listening to the answers. But that rocky, uneven ground is where spiritual growth lies.

Information is all well and good as far as it takes us, but when it comes to spiritual growth, it can't take us all the way. Information provides a necessary foundation, but we can be too quickly seduced into thinking it's all-sufficient. Good questions open up the issues people are really wondering about and prompt them to engage with God, helping them move toward growth and getting at the deeper issues beneath the information.

JENN

I've found that sometimes when I engage with God I'm not asking him the right kinds of questions. When I was in my corporate job and trying to transition into a career as a life coach, I was running into obstacles that would have been so easy for God to remove. The questions I was asking God at the time were, "Can you help me find part-time work? Can you lead me to twelve new clients so I can know all of my expenses will be covered? Can I get a paid assignment with my church?" An affirmative answer to any one of these questions would have provided me with assurance that I would be able to pay my bills. And yet they all led nowhere. The answer was always the same: "No." As the date I'd set as a goal to leave my corporate job approached, I became more and more anxious. I desperately wanted a financial safety net. I remember spending one morning confessing my fears and the ways I was lacking in faith. On the way to work that morning, I finally asked the right question: "Is this about me learning to trust you more by taking a leap of faith?" And the answer was clearly yes.

TEACHING VERSUS FACILITATION

Questions require faith. They require faith for us to ask them, and they require faith that someone will respond, whether that someone is God or the people in our small group. When we throw out a question to our group, we need to trust the people who are there. We need to trust them to engage and to look within themselves to find thoughts, insights and experiences that will help further the discussion.

One way to frame the difference between asking questions and making statements is facilitation versus teaching. Teaching is providing information and making statements designed to train or educate. Facilitation is asking questions that provide a structure for discussion. Think again of the function of the banks of the river. The banks don't control the water, but they provide certain parameters and direction. Facilitators act as river banks by providing direction and focus while moving things along.

Facilitators excel when they take a three-pronged approach to their role. They *expect* everyone to participate, *protect* people and their ideas, and *respect* others' viewpoints and time. Focusing in these areas builds trust and openness in the group. Feelings and reactions are explored and feedback is encouraged. This style of leadership does not lean on charisma, a seminary degree or expertise. It relies on a heart willing to listen to the Holy Spirit, to engage people and to believe everyone has something important to contribute.

We've noticed that people in many nontraditional churches don't respond very well to small groups in which someone teaches week after week. And we respond even less to fill-in-the-blank Bible studies. Perhaps we find these forms of learning to be condescending or dull, or we are too cynical to engage in growth in these formats. On the flip side, many great potential facilitators shy away from the "small group leader" role for fear they'll be expected to teach. By focusing on questions, facilitation pleases both parties. And, given that this format results in a more relational experience, facilitation skills are more helpful than teaching skills in guiding a group toward interactive learning and relationships with each other and with God.

Expect everyone to participate
(Remember: still waters run deep—some people need encouragement to participate.)

- *Use names.*

- *Maintain eye contact.*

- *Poll: "That's a great question; I'd like everyone to answer it."*

- *Ask powerful questions: "How could we move that a level deeper?"*

- *Ask personal questions: "What is the hardest thing for you to bring to this group?"*

- *Get feedback from the group: "What would you like more or less of from the group?"*

Protect people and their ideas

- *Acknowledge people's viewpoints: "I see your point" or "You have a point."*

- *Seek clarification: "I think you are suggesting ___; is that correct?"*

- *Intervene in order to respect differences of opinion: "Not everything is black and white. This is a tough issue and there area many different perspectives on it, even among Christians."*

- *Compare and contrast viewpoints: "How does that compare to what Alice said a moment ago?"*

- *Protect from interruptions: "I believe we might not have given Tom the chance to complete his thought. Tom, did you have more to say about that?"*

Respect others' time

- *Bring the group back on track: "There are a lot of different directions we could go with this. Let's go back to ___."*

- *Summarize often: "We've covered a lot of ground; would someone please summarize for us?"*

- *End on time: "We're reaching the end of our time together. I hate to cut off this great discussion, but let's pick up here next week."*

PRACTICE, PRACTICE, PRACTICE

We've intentionally designed this chapter not to be information-heavy. It's one thing to tell someone, "Ask open-ended questions," and quite another to ask them to sit down in groups and do it, and practice and collaborate on it. That's where the real learning takes place—when we can see and experience how questions lead us deeper into the realm of reflection, dialogue and a bit of wrestling, but with the ultimate purpose of knowing God better and more intimately.

Growing in our ability to ask good questions will take place mostly in the realm of the experiential: learning how to form good questions and asking them in the context of community. We begin with a bit of information, trust that the Holy Spirit will guide, and then practice, practice, practice in the context of community.

EXERCISES AND REFLECTION QUESTIONS

Exercise 1

Choose any passage of Scripture, and write out three or four open-ended questions that could be used to help people begin dialoguing with each other about the passage. The goal is to create questions that will encourage people to engage with the passage and will give them a platform to express their thoughts.

Going deeper. Repeat this exercise with other, more challenging, verses. Branch out in your passage selection. Sometimes the lesser-known passages can be easier and more productive because we have a lack of "right answers" at the ready.

Exercise 2

After a meaningful or difficult conversation with a friend or spouse, journal about all of the questions that were asked. What do you notice about the types of questions you ask? How often did you ask a question without an agenda or preconceived answer? What was the ratio of the number of questions you asked versus the number you were asked? Which questions did you think were best and why? Which questions took you deeper into your heart and into reflection?

Reflection Questions

1. When has someone asked you a truly powerful question? What was the result?

2. Identify someone in your life who is prone to provide you with advice and answers rather than asking questions. How do you feel about this? What request do you have of the person?

3. Think of a time when you've asked a question and then were irritated when someone answered it? What was going on in that interaction?

4. What's a topic that God might want you to wrestle with?

5. What is the question you tend to ask God most frequently? Is there a better or different question you might ask?

6. What are the questions that you believe your small group would most benefit from being asked?

7. What questions do you have for members of your group that would most help you understand who they are and what they need from the group?

5

ROCKS IN
THE RIVERBED

Navigating Group Conflict

*If a brother or sister sins, go and point
out the fault, just between the two of you.
If they listen to you, you have won
them over. But if they will not listen,
take one or two others along, so that
"every matter may be established by the
testimony of two or three witnesses."
If they still refuse to listen, tell it to the
church; and if they refuse to listen
even to the church, treat them as
you would a pagan or a tax collector.*

MATTHEW 18:15-17

The Bible is filled with conflict. You can read the Old Testament for some really good ones: Tamar and Judah, Cain and Abel, Jonah and God, Samson and Delilah, Moses and the Israelites, David and Absalom. One of the more well-known New Testament conflicts occurs between Paul and Barnabas (Acts 15:36-40). We touched on this story in the "Negotiating" section of chapter two. This conflict serves as a particularly good example for small groups since Paul and Barnabas had a close relationship. They were on the same side, the same team. They believed in the same vision. They went way back—Barnabas had guided Paul as he got started in ministry. But they still had a disagreement that turned into a conflict. Though Mark had deserted them on a previous journey, Barnabas wanted to take him along with them on another missionary journey. Paul disagreed.

Paul, true to his nature, dove head first into the conflict. He didn't sidestep or minimize his feelings about being deserted by Mark, not even for the sake of harmony. The result was a missions team split. They each chose a partner and went in different directions. As sometimes happens, things worked out for the best in spite of them—others joined the mission and more people were reached because there were now two teams rather than one.

But the best thing about this story is its ending. As we know from Paul's later letters, Mark, once disgraced but now proven and trustworthy, serves with Paul again (see 2 Timothy 4:11). We don't know what happened in the interim, but reconciliation and forgiveness have taken place.

Just like in the Bible, our small groups are rife with conflicts. Any small groups pastor will tell you that for every facilitator coming in with theological questions or problems, ten come in with interpersonal problems. Sometimes the conflict doesn't even wait for the formal group discussion to begin.

A FEW YEARS BACK I WAS COLEADING A SMALL GROUP with my husband, Mark, and we had reached the point where the group members were starting to get to know each other pretty well. Although we had only been meeting for about three months, people had shared personal things and it seemed like the group was beginning to bond. This particular night Mark was out of town, but I felt pretty confident leading the group myself. We usually had snacks in the kitchen and socialized for a while before moving to the living room and starting our discussion.

During the snack time, an argument broke out. The war in Iraq had just begun, and political feelings were running high on both sides. Two of the strongest personalities in the group—both of them very bright and very stubborn—found themselves on opposite sides of the issue, unable to understand how anyone else could possibly think differently. The argument started to escalate and pretty soon everyone else had stopped their conversations and was listening. Their voices started getting louder. I thought, *Oh no. I'm not sure what to do. I'm the only facilitator here tonight—we haven't even started the discussion yet—but I bet people expect me to do something. And this argument doesn't look like it's going to end of its own accord anytime soon. How should I handle this? I want to communicate that it's okay to talk about the tough issues, but this is really escalating and I want to be sure we're respectful of each other's opinions.* I looked around trying to read everyone's expressions, but they just looked stunned. I remember thinking, *Thank God there are no new people here tonight!*

So I started playing referee a bit, just saying things like, "Let him finish," whenever anyone got interrupted. By doing that, I had exerted some authority and let the rest of the group know that I was handling the situation. After about ten minutes of this, when I felt like both people had made their major points (although energy-wise they were just picking up steam at that point), I cut in and said, "I'm glad you feel comfortable talking about such a tough issue. . . . This is reality; I know this is on a lot of our minds, and we aren't here at this group just to be nice and pretend we agree even though we don't. I don't want to shut down this discussion, because I think it's important that we are able to talk about these kinds of things and hear other perspectives. However, it's past time we got started, and I want to honor that time as well. So how about we pick up this discussion and continue dialoguing after group."

We walked silently into the living room—there was a lot of tension. We always started our group with a check-in about where everyone was at and what kind of week they'd had. A few of the people who weren't involved in the argument shared first, and by the time it got around to one of the people who was involved, she apologized for some of the ways she'd handled the argument. She still felt strongly about her position, but regretted some of the ways she'd handled things. The other person apologized too. You could feel the tension in the room dissipating.

Although neither of the people involved in the argument has changed their political position, they did go on to become good friends. (They and their spouses even watched the presidential debates together the next election year—ill-advised but relationally brave.) That evening became a turning point in the group as well. It helped everyone realize that this was real life, we were going to be real here, and even if they thought differently on something, they'd be treated with respect by the group.

O   O   O

We've all heard many clichés and advice about conflict: Don't go to bed angry. Agree to disagree. Take a time out. Do unto others as you would have them do unto you. Forgive and forget. Seek first to understand. Some of this advice can be good and helpful in resolving conflict. However, the unspoken goal in most of it appears to be helping us *move past* what's uncomfortable about conflict rather than inspiring us to *move toward* what's uncomfortable about conflict for the sake of redemption, deeper commitment or intimacy.

DO THIS

When you sense tension between two people in your small group, take a proactive step and ask them (separately) about it. If a conflict does exist, offer to facilitate a meeting to help them resolve the situation.

Conflict has a purpose. It is not something to be avoided or circumvented, but something to be walked through with a vision for what could be. Imagine a friendship or a marriage in which two people have been through difficult times together, fought hard, overcome challenges and come out on the other side, reconciled and still together. Then imagine a friendship or marriage in which there have always been blue skies and clear sailing. Which is stronger? Of course, the one that has been tested and strengthened by that testing. The same is true of small groups. Generally, the presence of conflict means the group is deepening.

Conflict has a purpose—it grows us, it deepens our relationships, it tests our strength and character, and leads us toward maturity. Of course, all of those wonderful, spiritual-sounding reasons don't make conflict any easier to deal with. Most of us would prefer to avoid it if possible.

I HATE CONFLICT. THE THOUGHT OF AN IMPENDING CONFLICT makes me want to stay home in my slippers and bathrobe and hide. I could draw the blinds and watch a movie. That sounds much better. I want to be liked. Right now, my stomach is churning at the thought of an impending "hard conversation" that is about to happen, and I know very well that it could easily turn into a conflict. I have another of these hard conversations coming up next week. The thing that gets me is that I initiated both of these, because I knew the issues needed to be addressed. But now that it's inevitable, I just want to run away and isolate myself. I hear those voices, *Why did you need to start this? You could have just let it lie.*

○   ○   ○

This chapter might be hard to get excited about. Most of the time we don't want to try to sort through our conflicts, so why would we need skills to help us do that? We tell ourselves it will work itself out. In fact, we continue to say to ourselves, *It's not really worth getting into anyway. Since it will never be resolved, well, it's better not to bring it up at all. Maybe no one else really noticed that ripple anyway. I certainly don't want to be perceived as being oversensitive. And really, I'm not very close to that person anyway so it doesn't matter.*

When we join small groups, we are expressing a desire for deeper community. We are making a commitment to develop relationships with others in the group. It does matter. Unresolved conflicts usually find an outlet in other destructive behavior: gossip, self-protection, hardness of heart, passive-aggressive behavior, sarcasm used to keep others at arms length. And permanent marks are left on the relationship or the group. Unaddressed conflict has a way of surfacing—it *will* find an outlet.

Like water flowing through a riverbed, conflict must find a way around, over or through the rocks in its path when things get rough. Little patches of foam appear on the surface. Rapids and undertows run beneath. Things seem peaceful for a while, then all of a sudden these rocks start appearing and getting in the way. Sometimes if the rocks are big enough, they shift the course of the river. Other times, they just create a temporary rough patch. The water has to shift and the rocks begin to smooth over time—each affects the other. And every once in a great while, a steep drop-off transforms the river into a waterfall. Rocks, rapids and waterfalls are a natural—and inevitable—part of the life of the river.

DO THIS

In your small group, spend time up front—preferably before a conflict arises—establishing an agreement for how conflicts between group members will be handled.

THE DIVINE OPPORTUNITY

What comes to mind when you hear the word *conflict?* If you're like most of us, you're not thinking, *Bring it on! I want to grow! I want fresh perspective and learning!* You're more likely thinking, *Bad. Conflict bad. Must avoid.* Or if it can't be completely avoided, usually because someone else won't give up his or her position, then we should deal with it just as quickly as we can. Even if that approach ends up skirting the issues a bit, isn't it for a good cause? Peace and harmony?

The word *conflict* means "to strike together," which implies a certain degree of discomfort—even pain. You might picture two rocks being struck together, creating sparks. Or a match struck against something, creating fire. Friction, sparks, the collision of hard surfaces. "As iron sharpens iron, / so one person sharpens another" (Proverbs 27:17). Being sharp is good. But being sharpened—well . . .

As unfun as conflict is, it's often God's chosen vehicle for forward movement anyway. It's into the pencil sharpener for us if we expect to be useful. Consider—when is the time in your life you've sensed the most growth, the most reliance on God, the most intimacy with him? Odds are, you're not thinking of a time when you had it all together. People in recovery from drugs or alcohol will almost invariably say that that time for them was shortly after they hit bottom. We feel God's presence and involvement most when our need for him is the strongest. Or more accurately, when we've been most aware of our need for him. The times when we rely on God most—and consequently grow the most—are almost always diametrically opposed to the times when things are going fine. When we don't have it together, it's like an invitation for God to be at work.

So where there's conflict in your small group, keep a lookout for God. He's almost certainly there somewhere, peeking out from behind a curtain, waiting for the pregnant moment, the ripest opportunity to engage us in his healing work of transformation and reconciliation.

HEALING AND SECOND CHANCES

Have you ever noticed how the people who annoy you the most always seem to show up in your small group? There's Mr. Successful Businessman who thinks he's all that. There's Pollyanna, who's so cheerful we can feel ourselves veering toward sarcasm just as a counterbalance. Then there's the guy who just likes to hear himself talk, even if it means repeating his one point five different ways.

You know what's even worse? It's quite likely that God put them there just for us. If we need maturing, there's nothing quite like a sharp rock in the riverbed to accomplish that. Not that the annoying people don't have their own issues to deal with. They almost certainly do. It's just that when we assume we know what those issues are, we're quite often wrong.

Sometimes it's a simple matter of being annoyed and learning how to deal with it well. How can we respond, both internally and externally, in healthy ways? Other times, small group interactions and relationships can cut much closer to the bone. God seems to have a way of allowing the same old wounds to be opened over and over again. People will show up with personalities or issues or patterns of relating that trigger us. Are we just getting over a recent rejection? People will reject us. Have we felt abandoned in significant ways? People will leave us. Whatever we're dealing with, it will find some way to show up at our small group.

DO THIS

Conflicts are often associated with old hurts. Understand your hurts (or the hurts of the people involved in the conflict) and how they relate to the conflict before addressing it.

Although painful, sometimes God is providing us with opportunities to deal with what we've so far not dealt with: opportunities to grow and mature in deep ways, opportunities for healing.

JENN

ONE DAY A FACILITATOR FROM A SMALL GROUP called me to ask how to handle a conflict that happened the previous night during her small group. The group had formed to study the Song of Solomon. After several weeks, a man in the group named Peter realized that the facilitator believed that premarital sex is a sin. He started questioning her about this during the group discussion.

From what I could tell, it sounded like the facilitator was gracious in explaining the biblical foundation of her beliefs. He challenged her on that explanation from the perspective of cultural differences and modern relevance. He brought up things he thought would explain the biblical admonition, such as lack of effective birth control and limited women's rights.

After a few minutes, another man in the group engaged in the debate by quoting Scripture and stating incredulously that the biblical stance on premarital sex as a sin was obvious. Period. A few others appeared rather uncomfortable and quiet. Someone tried to smooth over the situation with comments such as, "We're all entitled to our own opinion. Let's move on and get back to the study." Then the topic was changed and everyone parted ways pretending nothing happened.

After the study, the man who had said the Bible's stance against premarital sex was obvious approached the facilitator. He said he was disappointed with himself for being so abrasive and that he wished he'd handled the situation differently. He felt he did not show enough respect for Peter and had not attempted to lead him toward Christ.

Peter called the facilitator that week and told her he would not be returning to the group. She encouraged him to talk with one of the male pastors on staff, but he had already concluded that this small group wasn't a place for him.

I wish I knew what happened to Peter, but I don't. What I do know is how much the small group leader was challenged by this situation. She started rethinking her own leadership and conflict styles. She felt a sense of responsibility for Peter's leaving and wanted to reduce the chance of something like that happening again. She had a bold conversation with the group about what they could do to create a safer place for people who are still learning about the Bible. She became a better leader.

O   O   O

This scenario is pretty typical of how conflicts unfold in groups. The following model can be used to chart the stages of escalation of a conflict.

We start in relationship and harmony with another person with *no conflict*. This level involves open communication and people feel free to express different opinions as they arise.

Latent conflict occurs when a difference emerges that is interest-based. Interests are desires that have no effect on a person's self-concept (e.g., What book should we study in small group?). During latent conflict, the issue hasn't been raised with others. In Jenn's story, this happened the moment Peter realized he disagreed with the facilitator's viewpoint on premarital sex.

Problems to solve occurs when a person decides to express his or her concerns—people remain fairly focused on the problem and their interests. Concern is shown for the other person and the relationship. With Peter, this happened when he took the step of expressing his differing opinion to the group.

Problems to solve become a *conflict* if personal needs are not being met (e.g., the need to be heard or respected). Personal needs are defined as basic human desires that are tied to things such as *self-esteem, values, power, perceptions and feelings*. Suddenly the needs take precedence over the original problem. When Peter realized that not only was his opinion on premarital sex considered incorrect by the group, but that some people flat out refused to consider what he was saying, he likely felt ganged-up on, judged and perhaps disrespected.

The next stage is *help*. Here one person might ask someone else for help (or might complain bitterly about how he or she has been treated). Peter likely went to this stage after the small group that night—perhaps he called a friend or sibling to talk about it. The effectiveness of getting help depends on who the person turns to—it's much more likely to make a difference if the helper is a *neutral* third party who can focus on resolving the conflict.

When help is ineffective, one or both parties will likely proceed to *fight or flight*. They either try to defeat or escape. Peter chose flight. The violations of his personal needs had to be addressed in order to mediate the conflict effectively.

Depending on the outcomes of *fight or flight*, the conflict may progress to *war*. The conflict has a life of its own at this stage, and sustaining the conflict becomes more important than resolving it. We most commonly see this happen in fierce rivalries, divorces or political and religious wars, and only rarely in small groups. With each stage, the relationship is further severed and people move farther and farther away from each other (William A. Donohue, *Managing Inter-*

personal Conflict; Dudley Weeks, *The Eight Essential Steps to Conflict Resolution*).

THE STAGES OF ESCALATION OF CONFLICT

Although conflicts are usually not this linear, they do tend to escalate through these general stages. They may skip the first three stages and move immediately into conflict. Or they may never experience *help*

Differences: My needs are met, but my interests are being challenged.

Conflict: My personal needs* are not met and my self-esteem is threatened.

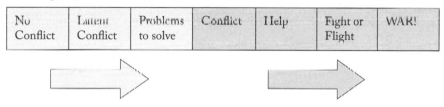

No Conflict	Latent Conflict	Problems to solve	Conflict	Help	Fight or Flight	WAR!

Personal needs refer to basic human desires that are tied to a person's self-esteem remaining intact. Included in personal needs are honoring a person's values, power, perceptions and feelings.

Figure 5.1. The stages of escalation of conflict

but rather jump to *flight*. Even though conflicts are not always linear, the goal in resolving them is to try to move to the previous stage, one stage at a time. For example, if parties in conflict address their personal needs, they will hopefully be able to refocus on their interests. In some cases they may discover that what they thought were personal needs were really just strong desires to have things their way.

So, let's take a breather and try to simplify: Differences surface. Statements are made. Assumptions are formed. Feelings are hurt. Sometimes the people involved agree to disagree. Other times they end with shouting or stony silence, each believing the other is in the wrong. Sometimes groups split or relationships end. Eventually, everyone moves on. Or do they? Just because the dialogue ends does not mean people have really moved on or let go of hard feelings. Even years later, when the details of the conflict are forgotten, the mistrust and the relational distance remain. Conflicts, even those that don't seem to be that severe, leave a mark. The mark may diminish over time, but somewhere in the subconscious there are questions. Is it safe to open up to her again? Is he harboring resentment toward me? Is it safe to take her out with my friends? Can I believe he really cares about me? Can we trust her to facilitate, given that she didn't handle that situation well? Most of the time everyone comes out feeling hurt and misunderstood, which is why it's so important for small group leaders to understand conflict and encourage reconciliation.

Conflict creates pressure, and it's tempting to try to wriggle out from under it. Working through it is never easy or smooth. We need to be committed to the process—and the relationships—in order to avoid running away and instead taking the hard steps of working it though. As one pastor we interviewed put it, "I want people on my team who will move toward me no matter what." He understands that if we are committed to the process, we can sometimes experience the healing work of God in our lives.

Tony and Cameron worked together on a church staff team for ten years. In many ways, they worked well together because their gifts, personalities, interests and perspectives were so different. Yet they'd butted heads many times over the course of those ten years as well. One time Tony, the senior pastor, scathingly criticized Cameron, an associate pastor. Tony's words cut deeply and stayed with Cameron for a long time. Instead of having their intended effect—"Do it better next time"—the criticism undermined Cameron's confidence and his performance declined. But the two men were relationally committed to each other and worked through the conflict, although it required several difficult conversations over the course of six months.

Fast forward two years. Tony and Cameron were in a meeting together and Tony was feeling stressed. Many things had not been going well lately. Although not directly criticizing Cameron, Tony made a few comments along the lines of "lack of momentum" and "not your strongest work," which created a sense of implied criticism in Cameron's mind. As Cameron was driving home, he found himself dwelling on the conversation, replaying parts in his mind. He was distracted

24-25 *You've all been to the stadium and seen the athletes race. Everyone runs; one wins. Run to win. All good athletes train hard. They do it for a gold medal that tarnishes and fades. You're after one that's gold eternally.* I Corinthians 9: 24 – 25 (from the Message Bible)

Each one of you has been such a blessing in my life and to this process of helping people run that race for the eternal gold!! I know you have helped me in my race. I pray that this book helps you continue in your journey of walking alongside others In that race.

May God continue to bless you and use you in this world to point people to Jesus Christ!!

Your friend and partner in ministry,

Todd

over dinner that night. Then he made a phone call to Tony. "I know we just met a few hours ago, but I don't want to sit and stew on this. When you said X, I heard you implying Y. Was that your intention?" And he opened the door to a conversation. They were committed to their friendship, to their working relationship and to working together on the staff team. They understood each other's issues, their own issues, and how those issues played off each other. That relational investment created the trust necessary for an open dialogue. The conflict resolved in less than ten minutes—or ten years and ten minutes, depending on how you look at it.

CONFLICT VERSUS DIFFERENCES

Similar to conflict—but different—are differences. We hope you'll have many, many differences voiced in your small group. Every week, if possible. Differences are what make things interesting and diverse. They're spirited, sometimes even competitive. We are certainly not expected to walk together in lockstep. There's a word for a small group in which everyone agrees with everyone else about everything. It's called a cult.

Differences are healthy—they help us determine who we are and what we believe. Let's take the example of what makes a church worthy of our attendance, volunteerism and tithes. No church can be all things to all people. And differing opinions abound on what makes a church good. Most of those opinions stem from personal values, priorities and preferences. Differences like this can create productive discussion, provoke thought, promote dialogue, challenge assumptions and all manner of other wonderful things that help us reflect and grow.

Differences cross the line into conflict when the focus shifts from ideas to personal needs. That shift can take place when one person begins imposing his or her opinions, perspectives, or values onto another person. Or when someone's self-concept is being questioned. Or when someone perceives his or her power is being taken away or challenged. In other words, when things get personal. "That church is not worthy of your involvement, and I can't believe you don't see that!" At that point, it's personal. Someone is feeling disrespected, and a conflict ensues.

Generally speaking, differences exist in the realm of theology or decisions about the direction of the group, while conflicts reside in the realm of people, their hearts and emotions, their values and needs. To make it even more confusing, sometimes what we perceive as needs are merely wants. The clearest way to differentiate between the two is to remember that needs are essential to the well-being of a person, whereas wants are not (Dudley Weeks, *Eight Essential Steps*). Top all of this off with the uniqueness of each individual and his or her needs and values, and it's pretty remarkable that any two people can actually get along.

VALUES ADDED

In chapter one, subtitled "Knowing Yourself," we highlighted the importance of knowing our own values. When we have the words to describe our values and to recognize others' values, we're much better equipped to deal with conflict.

JENN

SHORTLY AFTER I BECAME A CHRISTIAN, I joined a small group through my church. It was a group of married and single women in their twenties and early thirties who were interested in reading books that explored Christian topics together. Although the leadership was very casual, we set some pretty strict guidelines about what our group was going to be about. It was a place for us to come together to learn about the character of God. It wasn't group therapy. We hoped community would come out of that too, but community was definitely not the main objective.

Three weeks after the group started, one of the women in the group went through a very emotional break-up with her boyfriend. In the weeks that followed, our small group time was completely enveloped by this woman's situation. She showed up every week in tears and took all of our time sharing with us what she'd been through that week. It got really messy—her ex-boyfriend was badgering her to get back together. She seemed more interested in leaning on us than exploring the relationship spiritually or using the situation to better understand God. This went on for a few weeks and the group encouraged her, but also reminded her of the purpose of the group and suggested that she meet with a few members of the group on another evening so the rest of the group could proceed with our pursuit of the knowledge of God. Attempts by several members of the group to arrange another time were unsuccessful. She was angry about this suggestion, felt ashamed and rejected, and thought we were being unsupportive. She and the group parted ways.

The woman in Jenn's story who was going through the break-up had strong values around being included and accepted. The other women had values around honoring the intent of the small group. These differences felt irreconcilable. Although the friendships that existed before the group remained intact, the differences were never completely reconciled even though everyone involved made an effort. One of the realities of conflict and being in community with others is that people will have varying values, as well as varying styles (both healthy and unhealthy) of resolving conflict. To the degree that people can come to a deeper understanding and acceptance of each other's values, groups will be able to resolve these types of conflicts.

Notice that the point of this story is not about who was right or wrong. *Right versus wrong is never the point of a healthy conflict*—even though we may argue as though it were when we're in the midst of one. The point is not right or wrong, getting our way, changing someone else's opinion or proving something to ourselves.

What is the point?

At our best, we engage in conflict to be heard, known, understood, valued or respected. At our worst (because we're all at least a little messed-up), we engage in conflict out of fear, anger, shame or self-righteousness.

By engaging in conflict we can grow, learn about ourselves and others, and heal from past wounds. Conflict can also lead to deeper commitment to the other person, illustrated in our example of Cameron and Tony, because we are indirectly saying to them, "You are important to me. I am willing to deal with this disagreement so that it will not have a negative impact on our relationship." Or, "I will risk being perceived as oversensitive, arrogant or broken for the sake of a healthy relationship with you."

Counterintuitively, bringing a conflict to someone shows a deep level of respect for that person. After all, the issue could have simply gone unaddressed, allowing the relationship to fade with the sunset. The opportunity arises to value and connect with the other person in a deeper way. And often a more lasting bond is formed.

TARA

I MADE A CLOSE FRIEND IN A SMALL GROUP. We were close during some difficult seasons of our lives, but after a few years she moved across town. It was a forty-five-minute drive—not enough to feel long distance, but enough where our natural points of connection ceased. She no longer attended our small group or our church because of the distance. I wanted to keep in touch, but knew that my friend was quite busy with two small children. I called periodically, and tried to get together once in a while, but our meetings became less and less frequent. Some calls were unreturned, and I felt hurt.

I recognized that at this point, I had a choice. I could either let go or I could tell her how I felt. Opting for the latter, I sent her a brief e-mail letting her know I missed her and felt hurt that my calls had been unreturned. She wrote back, upset that I had addressed a conflict via e-mail. (One of the cardinal rules of conflict resolution is to never address a conflict via e-mail.) My e-mail had caught her off-guard, and she felt I didn't understand the current stresses of her life. I returned that I had tried to call, but couldn't get hold of her so e-mail was my only option.

We were both angry with each other for a while, but we got together to talk it through. Eventually we were able to move to a deeper level and reiterated that we valued and trusted one another. In a sense, the conflict only existed because I valued her (otherwise I would have let the relationship go) and I trusted her (otherwise I would not have brought a conflict to her).

To bring reconciliation and forgiveness, open dialogue is essential. Someone must take the risk to bring things to the table, to clear the air, even when it's scary.

Aliah was facilitating a small group that was doing a phenomenal job of reaching people normally outside the borders of the church. The group was fun, welcoming, warm and embracing. Deep relationships formed. Growth was evident. People overcame doubts and suspicion about church and were able to find Jesus in this intentionally accepting and nonchurchy small group. But after a while, some people in the group became uncomfortable with the level of looseness. They wanted to see less alcohol at social functions and less flirting and innuendo. The disagreement grew over time and invisible walls began to form within the group.

Aliah listened to the suggestions from the camp that wanted change. She could understand their perspective, but her vision for the group was more focused on reaching those who didn't know Christ than meeting accepted standards. To her mind, imposing rules was exactly the opposite of what this group was about. But instead of allowing the disagreement to turn into an unspoken conflict, Aliah decided to address the issue at a group meeting one night. She was understandably afraid. Would this discussion drive away the very people she wanted to reach? So many of them already believed that church groups were stuffy and legalistic, more concerned about enforcing rules than about loving one another. Would the night's meeting serve to reinforce the stereotype?

With much trepidation, Aliah facilitated an open forum. The group heard the concerns of those who wanted a less loose atmosphere and was given the chance to respond. People were respectful of one another, even in cases where they disagreed. Not everything was ironed out that night, and some disagreement still exists, but by Aliah's choice to bring the issue out into the light, the conflict was pushed backward into the realm of respectful disagreement. The damaging effects of conflict were robbed of their power as the conflict was deescalated. Aliah's courage opened the door to deeper understanding and reconciliation.

DO THIS

Before addressing a conflict, take time to gather your thoughts and composure. Breathe deeply and get centered so you can enter the conversation calm and grounded.

The best leaders and facilitators do not avoid hard conversations, tempting as that may be. After all, it's so much easier to choose not to engage when there's a difference of opinion. With engagement, we run the risk of appearing heavy-handed, insecure, weak, controlling, needy or wrong.

When we can see beyond the fear and the awkwardness of the moment, we can catch a glimpse of the larger vision: the transformation and redemption that are possible. Offering a space for people to deal with the things that lead to conflict—be it their twisted views of the Trinity or the pain that lurks stubbornly in their hearts—brings new life. When we see our groups as having a purpose much larger than their reputation, a purpose directly connected to the kingdom of God, we become more willing to risk conflict and walk through it. Because we know there is something on the other side. Something of value that we can't get to any other way.

MATTHEW 18

A passage that is most often quoted in the context of church discipline can also be helpful in resolving conflict. In fact, the whole conflict-resolution model presented later in this chapter is based on these verses.

> If a brother or sister sins, go and point out the fault, just between the two of you. If they listen to you, you have won them over. But if they will not

listen, take one or two others along, so that "every matter may be established by the testimony of two or three witnesses." If they still refuse to listen, tell it to the church; and if they refuse to listen even to the church, treat them as you would a pagan or a tax collector. (Matthew 18:15-17)

If someone wrongs us, or if we believe they've wronged us, we are to tell them. We are to try to work it out with them first, and later involve others only if necessary. It really is that simple. However, simple does not necessarily mean easy. That first step of telling someone directly when we feel wronged is a tough one. Generally the scenario runs more like this: we feel someone has wronged us, we tell someone else, they take our side, we feel better, the others form a negative opinion about the wrongdoer, hearts are hardened and unspoken barriers are built. Several variations of this pattern exist, but it's often that first step that trips us up: addressing the problem first just between the two of you. So that's the course we need to chart.

CHARTING A COURSE

NAVIGATING ROUGH WATERS IS UNPREDICTABLE by its very nature. I took my first rafting trip on the Colorado River through Westwater Canyon. My friend had prepared me for a thrilling adventure with lots of discussion about Class III and IV rapids. I pictured us strapped into our orange life preservers with waves crashing over our heads, soaking wet, bracing ourselves for the moment we might be tossed overboard, frantically bailing water out of the raft.

And it was a little bit like that, for a few minutes here and there. My friend was tossed out of the ducky near the daunting "Skull Rapid" and had seconds to dive back into the main raft. But the other seventeen miles of the trip were really quite calm and, at times, even a little boring for me. What I had built up as a risky adventure turned into a pretty relaxing time taking in the canyon views with some friends. But how might that experience have been different if we were with a guide who wasn't informed about the best way to hit each rapid? Or didn't know the impact of the water level that season? The guide's knowledge had made the experience of navigating rough waters more predictable.

Engaging in conflict means preparing for the unpredictable. But by preparing, we can sometimes help it go a little bit smoother. One helpful way of preparing is by taking the time beforehand to understand our natural tendencies. People tend to deal with conflict in five major ways. All options are available to anyone—we don't have just one pre-programmed response we're stuck with. And all of the options have their pros and cons. The key to engaging and resolving conflict successfully is determining which style is most appropriate in which situation and then applying it well.

- *Integrating.* Integrating involves reaching a decision that addresses the concerns of all parties and looks at the whole picture prior to reaching a solution. This style is helpful when the people involved will have regular contact in the future. It's also effective when the conflict involves complex issues. On the other hand, integrating also presents the most difficult and time-consuming approach to resolving conflict. It requires open communication, sharing facts and feelings, checking assumptions and seeing others' perspectives. This approach can work well in a small group where those involved are committed to the group and to the process. A group that disagrees on who to ask to replace the cofacilitator would be best served by getting the key people together to talk about their options and discern where God is leading them. They could meet, voice concerns, clarify misunderstandings and try to arrive at an agreement or consensus. The importance here is that people feel that their opinion is considered.

- *Compromising.* Compromising involves reaching an acceptable solution—giving up something to get something. It's a tradeoff. Compromise can be most useful when both parties have reached an impasse, as it will bring at least some satisfaction to all. A group that disagrees about what topic to study could decide to trade off every other week or to do one study first and the other study next.

- *Competing.* Competing brings with it a win-lose mentality. This adversarial approach involves standing one's ground and not giving in on the issues. If no long-term relationships are at stake and your concern needs immediate attention, competing may be a good option. It's the approach favored for buying an automobile or defending a legal problem in court. But competing is rarely a productive strategy for resolving conflict in a small group because of the relational context.

- *Smoothing.* Giving in or accommodating the needs of the other person at the expense of one's own needs is called smoothing. Going along for the sake of harmony and agreement. Smoothing is a temporary fix. It may be useful when moving the conflict to a new level, such as accepting the excuse a cofacilitator makes after showing up late for the last four small groups, but then choosing to take time later to address their lack of commitment to the group. Smoothing can also be effective when a new visitor attends and presents opinions vastly different from the rest of the group.

- *Avoiding.* Avoiding involves withdrawing from a potential conflict, sidestepping it or keeping divergent opinions to oneself. If someone is rude to you at the airport, you might as well let their comment roll off and avoid the conflict altogether—you likely have little to gain by trying to put them in their place. In small group settings, sometimes you may need to pick your battles. If there are several potential points of conflict, you may choose to ignore some in order to address the more strategic, underlying issue. For example, don't bite the hook of engaging in numerous theological debates with a group member who really needs to be confronted on always needing to be right. Other conflicts may work themselves out over time and are better off left alone. And some may be irresolvable, such as a conflict that stems from fundamentally different personal values or worldviews.

(Adapted from Kenneth W. Thomas and Ralph H. Kilmann, *The Thomas-Kilmann Conflict Mode Instrument*)

Most of us have a favored style for resolving conflict—a default. If we know our default as well as the other options, we'll have a full stockpile of resources at our disposal.

JENN

I REALLY LIKE TO BELIEVE MY DEFAULT IS INTEGRATING because it seems the most relational, but the truth came out shortly after Sammy and I got married—I default to competing. I take the stance that I am right and if he had all of the facts he'd surely agree with me. When I believe I am absolutely right or have justified myself to the nth degree, that's the clearest indication I'm stuck in my default and likely have something to learn. In other words, the more I analyze the speck in his eye, the more likely it is that there's a log in my own—and that God's trying to develop something in me.

○   ○   ○

Know your defaults. And know that it can be very easy to talk yourself into believing that your default is the best option in any given situation. For example, let's say Gene's default is *avoiding*, and trouble begins brewing in his group. Likely, he'll ignore it for a while as it gets worse. When it reaches the boiling point and can no longer be ignored, there's likely to be an outburst of some kind. Let's say Chad lashes out at him or criticizes him sarcastically. Based on that outburst, Gene very likely may be able to convince himself that, clearly, this conflict is irresolvable, so engagement should not be attempted. He may tell himself that Chad is an unsafe person and cut himself off emotionally. Or Gene may inappropriately employ smoothing as a way of not dealing with the issue. Likely, any of these approaches will serve only to infuriate Chad further.

Choosing to step outside of our comfort zones and learn to handle conflict in different ways can have a tremendous effect on all of our significant relationships. John Gottman's extensive research revealed that the way conflict is approached in a marriage relationship predicts whether the marriage will succeed or fail. Let's clarify—that's not just *one* of the factors to consider—it's *the* factor, the predictor that determines success or failure. How we handle conflict matters.

WORKING AT CONFLICT

So how do we learn? How do we grow and change?

1. *Self-awareness*. Think back again to the chapter one, where we discussed "knowing yourself." The greater our self-awareness, the better we'll be at handling conflict. What do you notice when you're in conflict? Do your emotions flood you and make it impossible for you to think or act rationally? Do you stonewall the person to punish or control them? Do something passive-aggressive? Try to turn the table on them by recalling something they did last month? Do whatever you can to get reassurance they still like you?

Perhaps we notice a bunch of catastrophic or damning thoughts about ourselves floating around in our heads. Where did those thoughts come from? Studies show that during difficult conversations women are more likely to have thoughts generated by fears: she's not going to want to be my friend anymore, my job is at risk, he's not attracted to me anymore. Men are more prone to shame: she doesn't think I'm capable, my boss has figured out I am a poser, he's disappointed with me (see Patricia Love and Steven Stosny, *How to Improve Your Marriage Without Talking About It*). Some of each makes an especially lovely combination—and seems specially

DO THIS

Devote one of your small group gatherings (or even a series of them) to exploring conflict and forgiveness. Ask each person there to share about a recent conflict in his or her life. Help the person to understand the stage of the conflict and his or her conflict styles. Ask the person what the next step toward reconciliation and forgiveness might look like. Hold a follow-up discussion later to let people share stories about the effect of the steps they took.

designed to move us in the least productive direction possible. However, the more we can be aware of those negative defaults and self-defeating thoughts, the more we'll be able to make more clear-headed choices about how to respond.

Counting to ten, taking a few deep breaths, or stepping outside for a minute can give us the space we need to connect with what's really going on. Research shows that feelings associated with conflict—such as frustration, anger and anxiety—cause the neural activity in the two branches of the autonomic nervous system to get out of sync. This disruption of the synchronized activity in the brain affects our ability to think clearly. It takes just fractions of a second to get out of sync. The space between "It's probably not a good time for me to talk about this" and spewing on and on about what we'd just decided we shouldn't discuss can be surprisingly short. Asking the other person for just a few minutes can make a world of difference in the outcome.

2. *Reflection*. Below are some questions we can ask ourselves while we're getting back in sync or after we've had a little more time to reflect.

- On a scale of 1-10, how strongly do I feel I'm right? (10 being 100 percent convinced)
- On a scale of 1-10 how important is it that I am right?
- What is this conflict *really* about?
- To what degree can I see the other person's perspective?
- Can I verbalize the other person's perspective (in a nonsatirical way)?
- What is my perceived need? Is this really a need, or is it a want?
- What's my default in how I handle conflict?
- In what situations is my default most helpful? In what situations is it least helpful? Is this one of those situations?
- What assumptions am I making?

3. *See through different eyes.* We can also try out some of the other options—the ones that don't come so naturally to us. If we usually fight our point to the death, why not try compromising on this one? If we usually smooth or avoid, maybe we could try the daunting task of integrating. It's a matter of trying to discern which method might be the most effective given the situation. And recognizing we aren't limited to our usual repertoire. Trial—and even error—can be eye-opening.

People who are different than us are our best resources. They can provide different perspectives, challenging the lenses we are accustomed to viewing the world through. Open conversations about how we deal with conflict, when it works and when it doesn't, can open up new learning and perspectives. As in most areas of life, we can learn a great deal from those who are different than us.

THE TOOL

When we've led facilitator trainings in the area of conflict, the most common request is for a tool. "Something I can take and use," the desperate facilitators request, "something that will help me deal with the conflict in my group." The bad news is there's no magic bullet. There is no tool or approach that will ensure that it comes out all right in the end. Conflicts are too varied, too messy and too people-based for that. However, the good news is that there are some general communication principles that can be adapted and applied to various situations.

So here's our best shot at a tool based on those principles—we call it the feedback model because it basically facilitates the flow of feedback by structuring the conversation. As a facilitator, this approach can be especially helpful if others turn to you to mediate a conflict. The goal of using this tool is to help others move backward through the stages of a conflict, deescalating it.

Sometimes a counter-proposal may be made that creates a hybrid solution. For example, the other person may ask that the group start-time be pushed back fifteen minutes because he or she is consistently running into traffic.

Table 5.1. Feedback Model for Conflict Resolution

Stage One: Dos & Don'ts	During this stage the parties set ground rules for the conversation (e.g., no interrupting, no yelling, try not to react, try not to be defensive, take five when needed to manage emotions, etc.).
Stage Two: Cards on the Table	Next, everyone puts their cards on the table. The people involved take turns responding to the following three steps, one at a time: 1. Describe the behavior that led to conflict. 2. Describe the impact on you—what "need" isn't being met? 3. Make a request—generate possible solutions. People are not given an opportunity to respond to the other, but rather to express their perception of what happened and the impact. Responding to the other may or may not be necessary, but it typically results in debate or defensiveness and can easily become counterproductive. The goal here is for the people involved to connect to and understand each other's feelings, even if they have a different perception of the situation. This understanding serves to establish trust and encourage openness.
Stage Three: We Can Work It Out	During this stage, the people involved select a solution based on the options that have been suggested or an integrated solution. Confirm the agreement at the end of the discussion to make sure there are no misunderstandings.
Stage Four: Kiss & Make Up	At this point, people validate each other to develop a common ground of care and respect.

Ending with validation—the kiss-and-make-up stage—is easy to let fall by the wayside. But never underestimate the power of validation. A sincere reminder of our strengths after a conflict serves to strengthen the relational bond. "What you bring to the group is so valuable—your insights and perspectives help us to go to deeper places. I am so glad we worked through this and will continue to serve together."

For an additional tool, see also "What to Do with a Conflict" in appendix five. This tool, based on Matthew 18, provides reminders of some practical things to consider before addressing a conflict, potential steps to take toward resolving the conflict, and a few considerations if you're helping mediate a conflict between others.

RESOLUTION VERSUS FORGIVENESS

Generally the goal of dealing with conflict is to find a resolution. That's a good goal—certainly better than harboring unacknowledged anger or just leaving. Yet there are different kinds of resolution. There's a kind of resolution that functions as a legal contract or a treaty: I do this, you do that, and we'll live at peace. Better than war, certainly, but quite a distance from the vision of the kingdom of God. Someday . . . someday when the fullness of the kingdom comes, we'll have not just treaties or contracts but true reconciliation, renewal of relationship, a fresh start between us and God, and between us and others.

> Then I saw "a new heaven and a new earth," for the first heaven and the first earth had passed away, and there was no longer any sea. I saw the Holy City, the new Jerusalem, coming down out of heaven from God, prepared as a bride beautifully dressed for her husband. And I heard a loud voice from the throne saying, "Look! God's dwelling place is now among the people, and he will dwell with them. They will be his people, and God himself will be with them and be their God. 'He will wipe every tear from their eyes. There will be no more death' or mourning or crying or pain, for the old order of things has passed away."
>
> He who was seated on the throne said, "I am making everything new!" Then he said, "Write this down, for these words are trustworthy and true."
>
> He said to me: "It is done. I am the Alpha and the Omega, the Beginning and the End. To the thirsty I will give water without cost from the spring of the water of life." (Revelation 21:1-6)

So in the meantime, until the coming of the kingdom in all its fullness, we have tastes, glimpses of that kingdom. True forgiveness and reconciliation is a glimpse of the coming kingdom, of the face of God.

Again, not just conflict to be gotten around or gotten through, but conflict for the sake of the richness of the forgiveness, growth, reconciliation and redemption to be had on the other side.

Biblical forgiveness is really hard to do. Sure, it's easy to talk about. And it's easy to understand why Jesus tells us to forgive those who sin against us seventy times seven. Harboring unforgiveness destroys the soul. Even from a strictly selfish perspective, it's better to forgive. We can avoid a lot of bitterness, fear and pain that way. Most people and religions agree that forgiveness is virtuous.

But even if we agree with all of the logic behind Jesus' directive, *actually* forgiving someone is another matter. What if the person isn't repentant? What about all of the anger and emotions? Do we pretend they don't exist? What's the difference between resolution and reconciliation? And what about damaged trust?

To make forgiving others even more complicated, we have an amazing capacity to convince ourselves that we've forgiven people when we really haven't. "Yes, I have forgiven her. I just don't know if I want a relationship with her anymore." Sometimes that can be true. But much of the time that desire to run indicates forgiveness isn't fully experienced. It doesn't always lead us into what God desires for us: freedom.

JENN

WHEN I (FINALLY) MADE A CHOICE TO FORGIVE someone who had deeply hurt me, I experienced closeness to God that was almost as significant as when I first became a believer. All of my head knowledge about forgiveness and about God's grace toward me became real in my heart. The person graciously said to me recently, "It was your willingness to forgive me that allowed you to play a major role in putting me on the road to restoration." We both experienced freedom.

○   ○   ○

In our groups, when we share stories with each other about how God has changed our hearts and made forgiveness possible, it helps others move toward forgiveness, often much more powerfully than logical arguments and glibly quoted Bible verses. Real forgiveness helps us realize that our unanswered questions about repentance and reconciliation aren't as important as we thought.

The biggest myth about forgiveness is that it is something we do primarily for the sake of the other person. That is not true. It is done primarily for us. We

DO THIS

Discuss Matthew 5:23-24 and the implications of this passage for your small group:

Therefore, if you are offering your gift at the altar and there remember that your brother or sister has something against you, leave your gift there in front of the altar. First go and be reconciled to that person; then come and offer your gift.

are forgiven by God. And when, remembering our own forgiveness, we forgive others, that is done for our sake as well. Holding resentment in our hearts harms us much more than the person we are intending to harm. The path of forgiveness leads us through hurt, disillusionment, letting go of expectations, and seeing the unique image of God in the other person. That path is neither easy nor immediate, but remains well worth traveling. We will never know freedom until we forgive and let go.

THE FREEDOM OF DISILLUSIONMENT

People are not what we expect. They are not as kind, as clever or interesting, as reliable, as unselfish as we had hoped. Disillusionment is an inevitable piece of being involved in a small group or a church for any length of time. Possibly that is why we keep moving on. Surely it—the perfect group, the perfect church—will be there, around the next bend, in the next group, in the next church. But somehow, it isn't.

Dietrich Bonhoeffer, whose time living in a communal setting with other believers taught him much about community, wrote:

Innumerable times a whole Christian community has broken down because it had sprung from a wish dream. The serious Christian, set down for the first time in a Christian community, is likely to bring with him a very definite idea of what Christian life together should be and try to realize it. But God's grace speedily shatters such dreams. Just as surely as God desires to lead us to a knowledge of genuine Christian fellowship, so surely must we be overwhelmed by a great disillusionment with others, with Christians in general, and, if we are fortunate, with ourselves. Only that fellowship which faces such disillusionment, with all its unhappy and ugly aspects, begins to be what it should be in God's sight, begins to grasp in faith the promise that is given to it. The sooner this shock of disillusionment comes to an individual and to a community, the better for both. *(Life Together)*

Flora, a friend of ours, told us, "Many years ago, reading *Life Together* helped me stay in the church. I was so angry and disappointed when our church at that time turned out to be NOT 'The Friends of Flora.' But I did come to be more patient with 'The Friends of Jesus,' especially when I began to realize I was as hard for some people to tolerate as they were for me. I stayed at that church another twenty years."

LETTING GO

"Well," one might say, "that's all very well and good. But you don't understand the situation *I'm* in. This is really awful. How do I know whether it's time to move on?"

Sometimes Matthew 18 doesn't work. Sometimes we get stuck. Sometimes we develop a vision for something different. Sometimes we find we have something to give in a new context. And sometimes, even when things are hard, we need to stay and wait. Sometimes we need to work toward reconciliation. Listen. Discern.

What will bring you toward growth and maturity? Staying? Letting go? Moving on? Sometimes the answers can be found in our past. If an honest look at our history reveals that we bolt when we don't get what we want (even if we've come up with really good reasons for why we left), we are probably being asked to stay. Or maybe that honest look at our past indicates that we hold on too long, past when all hope is gone, out of fear of the unknown. Then perhaps we're being asked to let go and take the risk associated with new relationships. Reflection, prayer and the counsel of trusted friends can help us discern where the Spirit is really leading.

But whatever we might decide, we must hold on to the kind of "dis-illusionment" Bonhoeffer mentions. Another friend recently reflected, "Yes, my current situation is lonely, but it's revealed a deeper loneliness, which is the ache of all humanity for a true and deep connection, which, ironically, can't be met at all by another human. The hole is far too deep for that."

While small groups move people toward meaningful connection, our deepest connection must come ultimately from God. When we pursue the resolution of conflict, seeking reconciliation and forgiveness, not putting the burden of meeting all of our needs on others, we put ourselves in the best place to see God at work. From our position in the middle of human messiness, we can catch glimpses and tastes of the kingdom to come.

EXERCISES AND REFLECTION QUESTIONS

1. Small groups and their propensity for conflict are a lot like the edge of a particular stretch of highway described by John Steinbeck in *The Grapes of Wrath:*

   > The concrete highway was edged with a mat of tangled, broken, dry grass, and the grass heads were heavy with oat beards to catch on a dog's coat, and foxtails to tangle in a horse's fetlocks, and clover burrs to fasten to sheep's wool; sleeping life waiting to be spread and dispersed, every seed armed with an appliance of dispersal, twisting darts and parachutes for the wind, little spears and balls of tiny thorns, all waiting for animals and for the wind, for a man's trouser cuff or the hem of a woman's skirt.

   Like the side of this stretch of highway, there are entrapments and obstacles that exist in close community that are nearly impossible to navigate or avoid. But notice the description doesn't stop with the oat beards and foxtails and clover burrs—the potential for new life and transformation is waiting. Identify the entrapments and obstacles in your small group. Write a list. And then imagine the potential for new life. Dream about the possibilities of what could happen in the hearts of the people in your group. Also notice your perspective about the inevitable conflict your small group experiences. Do you view your small group as a field of traps? Threatening, inconvenient and uncomfortable? Or as "sleeping life waiting to be spread"? Life-giving and redeeming? What is the perspective you want to hold about conflict in your small group? How might you turn this perspective into commitment or action?

2. Think of a conflict that you currently have with someone. What is possible in terms of restoration? How might you make use of the tools referenced in this chapter?

3. Recall a time when you neglected to address hurt feelings with someone close to you. What was the effect?

4. Think of a conflict that you recently had with someone. What would have made the situation or interaction more powerful? (Use the reflection questions earlier in this chapter as a guide.)

5. What kind of person do you want to be when it comes to conflict? What are some things people in your small group appear to value that you don't? What will you do with these differences?

6. What is preventing you from addressing conflict in your group or other areas of your life?

7. What's your default style for resolving conflict? In what situations is your default style most helpful? In what situations is it most damaging?

8. What is a conversation you've been postponing or avoiding? Use the steps outlined in "The Tool" section of this chapter as a guideline.

9. Who might you need to forgive more completely? What will you do to move toward restoration?

6

CREATING
NEW STREAMS

Developing New Leaders

His master replied, "Well done,
good and faithful servant!
You have been faithful with a few
things; I will put you in charge
of many things. Come and share
your master's happiness!"

MATTHEW 25:23

Joyce once facilitated a prayer-based women's group. Prayer was a passion of hers and she was gifted in a way that drew others. Joyce was an older woman, comfortable with who she was, and she enjoyed using her shepherding gifts to encourage the younger women toward deepening their walk with God. After about a year, the focus of the group began shifting. Their prayer for the city in which they lived was leading them toward increased activism. Corporately, the women decided to get more actively involved in meeting needs in their community.

"I am really excited about this new direction," said Joyce. "It feels like it's of God, and a natural outflow from our times of prayer and reflection. I definitely want to be a part of this new phase. That said, I don't know that I'm the best person to continue in a facilitation role. I think you're going to need someone with a more direct leadership style, someone who can organize outings, cast vision, delegate responsibilities. That's just not me. And I can see this new direction challenging me in some really important ways, and I think I need to be in a learner role to fully experience that."

Joyce, by stepping down from her role at just the right time, showed exemplary self-awareness, an understanding of the needs and direction of the group, and the ability to listen to the Holy Spirit. These qualities in a facilitator contribute toward empowering others and investing in their development.

DO THIS

Always maintain a relationship with someone in your small group who you are developing as a potential facilitator.

Sometimes rivers change their course, and a group needs a new leader to take it in a new direction. Sometimes rivers overflow their banks, and multiple leaders are needed to help navigate. Sometimes rivers branch off into two different streams, and different leaders are required for each. This can either be caused by hitting a rock (unresolved conflict) or as a natural response to the terrain (you guys are going this direction and we're going that, both of which are good). And, even if the cause was conflict, often the result is good. The more streams that branch off of an existing river, the more land that can be covered and nourished. During the natural course of group life, new leaders will be needed for all kinds of circumstances. We don't know what turns the river will take.

In this book we've used the term *facilitator* rather than *leader*. That's because facilitator seems to communicate better to most people the shared leadership style necessary for healthy small groups. However, in biblical leadership the emphasis is on serving, equipping and developing others. In that sense, leader and facilitator are almost synonymous. And truly, one of the most important tasks of a facilitator is to develop other leaders—leaders of all kinds.

A man named Patrick, who once led a rather large small group, refused the term *leader* outright. Instead, he insisted that he was just helping out with coordinating the group, and other people were really making it happen. And indeed, Patrick did have help. He had another person hosting. He asked different people to help with the teaching/content portion of the evening. He had set up an e-mail listserve so others in the group could initiate service projects. He designated prayer group leaders for the end of the evening, when prayer and sharing were done in smaller groups-within-a-group.

In short, Patrick was leading in the most biblical way possible—by developing others. He could quickly spot someone with a teaching or hospitality gift. He identified the people who had the shepherding gifts necessary to guide the prayer groups, where people felt included and heard. And whenever Patrick saw those gifts, he called them out by asking people if they would be willing to serve by using them. When people were ready to use their gifts, ownership was created. In this way, the group had developed enough traction that when Patrick was no longer available to lead, it continued on without him.

At a certain point, the time comes when we need to own the gifts God has given us. Not in order to say how great we are, or to have a power trip, or to have sole control of the group, but in order to glorify God and be a part of calling out his glory in others.

There is a great need out there for new leaders, people who are ready to step out and begin using their gifts to serve others. That need is built into the life cycle of groups; we will always need new facilitators and new groups because there are always more people to reach and to include in the kingdom of God. To the degree that we lack new facilitators and new groups, we stall in our ability to reach out and be inclusive to others.

Although it frustrates church staff members to no end, this is the way God seems to have set things up for ongoing ministry. Think about it—God could have made it so that we had an unlimited supply of qualified new leaders, just sitting there on the shelf (probably in cold storage) waiting for the time when a need should arise. Then, when

Kelly suggests that we really should offer a spiritual gifts class, or Joe notices that we could use some additional people to help lead worship, new leaders would be perfectly trained, available and ready to go. Although this sounds good—especially to most pastors—a church like this would actually be in really bad shape. It would be consumeristic (do my bidding and do it now!). It would be falling far short of its capacity for real ministry (imagine leaders sitting on shelves waiting for a way to be useful!).

DO THIS

Regularly give all of the people in your group opportunities to facilitate—even if it's something as simple as leading in a group ice-breaker—so you can observe their skills and give them a chance to develop and stretch.

But worst of all, there'd be no room in this church for the rest of us, the underdeveloped, the imperfect, the partially competent. What about Vincent, who suspects that he may have a teaching gift, but he's not really sure, and he'd like to teach that class on spiritual gifts, but he's afraid—what if he utterly messes it up? Vincent would be reduced to a pew-sitter in that kind of church.

If all of our churches had competent leaders whenever one was needed, we'd all be missing our call to grow toward maturity.

> *So Christ himself gave the apostles, the prophets, the evangelists, the pastors and teachers, to equip his people for works of service, so that the body of Christ may be built up until we all reach unity in the faith and in the knowledge of the Son of God and become mature, attaining to the whole measure of the fullness of Christ.*

(EPHESIANS 4:11-13)

This becoming mature, this attaining to the whole measure of the fullness of Christ, is one of the main points of the church, and it's a beautiful thing to be a part of when we see it happening. Not beautiful like a streamlined building of glass and steel, all smooth and shiny and reflecting back the sunlight unchanged, but beautiful like a rustic mountain cabin built by hand, where we can see the fingerprints in the mortar between the logs and someone put the chimney a little off-center, but boy did they choose some beautiful stones to make it out of. That kind of beautiful.

BEAUTIFUL FAILURE

That kind of beautiful is never fun in the making. Anyone who has ever bombed a sermon or put up the wrong PowerPoint slide in the middle of a song or said something truly regrettable in a small group knows that. Even years later, some of those scenes may be painful to recall. Usually what makes the memory of those events particularly painful are the responses of others. After the bombed sermon, did someone say to you, "Guess preaching's not your gift after all, is it?" or "Don't quit your day job just yet"? Did your team leader turn around and glare at you when you dropped the ball on the PowerPoint slide? Did someone in your small group tell you you're the most insensitive person they've ever met and they can't believe they brought a friend that night?

None of us are perfect. And none of us are competent when we start doing something new, no matter how easy it may be for someone else. We all have those memories of failure, the ones that make us wince when we think about them. Those are the memories we need to lean on when we are working with someone who is new to facilitating small groups. The key word here is *grace*.

SEVERAL YEARS AGO I WAS WORKING FROM HOME doing writing projects for an organization in another state. I was working on a big project and felt like I'd been making a lot of progress. My boss had mentioned when I started the job that I should back up my files periodically. Being rather computer illiterate, I thought the backup process seemed kind of complicated. Someone had showed me how to do it once, but I couldn't quite remember the steps. So I saved all of my work on the hard drive and sent sections to my boss periodically, thinking that should be sufficient. Eventually, I forgot all about backing up my files.

Then the inevitable happened. My computer crashed, and I lost all of my data—two weeks' worth of work that hadn't yet been sent on to headquarters. I had to tell my boss. I felt terrible. I thought I might get fired. Being a very gracious man, my boss didn't say any of the many things he would have been quite justified in saying. Instead, after asking a few informational questions about the extent of the problem and digesting what I had told him, he said—with a smile I could hear over the phone—"Well. The positive side is I don't think you'll ever make this same mistake again."

JENN

IN CONTRAST TO TARA'S STORY OF A LEADER REACTING well to her mistake, I once experienced the opposite. I was taking an oral examination in front of a panel of experts in my field. And, as if that's not daunting enough, when I entered the exam room my chair was positioned in such a way that I would be facing a large video camera being used to capture my performance—every word, every expression, every breath. As someone who is camera-shy and doesn't like the limelight, I now had stage fright to add to my stress. I stumbled through the first part of my presentation barely remembering the purpose of what I was doing or the principles behind it.

During a break before the second portion of my presentation, I went into the hallway to try to gain some composure. At that time one of the panelists came into the hallway to check on me. "How do you think it's going?" she said. Although this was a very good question, the way in which it was posed, her body language and the expression on her face indicated to me that she thought things went poorly. Based on my response she said, "Don't think that my decision to come talk to you has anything to do with what happened in there." To me this was just confirmation that I had totally botched up my presentation, and she was sent to try to hurry up and fix me before the second part of the presentation. "What do you need before you go back in there?" "Take as much time as you need." These comments, although well-intended, actually added to the pressure and I returned to the room for a repeat performance—I made all of the same mistakes again.

The vast majority of the time we don't have to be told when we've made a mistake or totally bombed. We know it. Or, in our insecurities, we believe it even when it's not true. Debriefing a small group session with a new leader can be done almost entirely through questions. What did you see going well? What contributed to that? What would you like to see different next time? What are some ways you could try to move things in that direction? Where are some areas where you'd like to grow? How did you feel about the evening in general? Again, being aware of body language and tone can help us avoid sending unintended messages.

It's seldom necessary to criticize or bring up the negative. And it's never necessary to try to fix them. The greatest way to develop someone is to communicate over and over how much you believe in them and how much you believe that they will learn from experience, both good and bad. That was the kind of confidence that Tara's boss showed in her.

It's not necessary to be critical. But sometimes, it will be necessary to say hard things. Those times will come infrequently, and should, so that when they do come, they're the exception rather than the rule. One group member had been pouring herself into others to such a degree that she was stunting her own growth. Susanne seldom allowed herself any time alone. She was being overly generous with her time and her money, at great expense to her family. Her various service projects were beginning to take a toll on her health and her marriage. The facilitator of her group, who had always been supportive and encouraging, told her, "You're giving too much." Susanne was furious. Who was he to say such a thing to her? He wasn't really around enough to know that. He didn't know what he was talking about. Her pride was hurt; so much of her identity came from serving others. After a couple days of stewing on his comment, Susanne came back to him and acknowledged, "I really needed to hear that."

Sometimes as we help develop others, we'll be called on to say what we see, even when we know it's not going to go well. And usually those comments aren't skills-oriented, like, "A better thing to say then would have been . . ." Usually they're centered around character, like "I noticed you brought things back to yourself a lot," because character is where we're all developing. And that's where we all need each other's eyes and ears. When we provide consistent support, the relationship is usually strong enough for those rare, hard-to-hear comments to be heard.

Think of the movies you've seen that depicted someone experiencing tremendous growth or overcoming great obstacles. Almost invariably, you'll also see someone alongside them who loves and invests in them. This archetypal theme can be found in many of the popular films of the last decade—*Good Will Hunting*, *A Beautiful Mind*, *Antwone Fisher*, *Seabiscuit*, *Cinderella Man*, *Million Dollar Baby* and many more. The relational investment is essential.

Developing others is a messy process. Learning anything new is messy. Would doing it ourselves be easier? Yes. But it wouldn't be better. We'd miss being a part of the messiness that is such an integral part of God's plan for building us up into the fullness of Christ.

TAKING NOTICE

In the 1970s movie *Kung Fu*, David Carradine's character meets an old martial arts master who is blind. Carradine expresses sympathy over the blindness, saying how hard it must be to not be able to see. The old master responds that he can see beyond what Carradine can: "Do you not see the grasshopper at your feet?" Carradine looks down, amazed that the blind old man noticed it before he did. And as a learner, Carradine's character is rechristened "Grasshopper."

In a way, that's our role in developing others; we can serve as someone who helps others take notice of their surroundings, their strengths and so on. Often we will notice things that people can't see about themselves and can reflect that back to them.

Every new leader needs a martial arts master. And as leaders become seasoned, they need a grasshopper. In between, it's not that we need neither—we need both. Most of us have things to learn as well as things to pass on. When viewed from a broader, more holistic perspective, the most important role of a group leader is not facilitating the group, it's developing more facilitators. If your own group ends, but you've developed two new facilitators, each of whom are leading a group now, you're ending up ahead. Facilitators need to look for other facilitators. Hosts need to look for other hosts. Whatever gifts we have, God calls us to help develop them in others.

TARA

WHEN I WAS IN GRAD SCHOOL IN MY MID-TWENTIES I attended a small group hosted by Debbie, a woman of about forty who became a mentor of mine. Over the course of a couple of years, I had a lot of different op portunities to watch her exercise her considerable hospitality gifts. She seemed comfortable with herself and with others in a way that made people relax and feel at home. I noticed she didn't feel the need to have her house white-glove clean. I noticed that she always had food and drinks going, that she never seemed in a hurry, that she let people help with dishes and get their own glasses out of the cabinet. She even let a bunch of students (myself included) have a food fight in her kitchen one night. Her house felt like home to a lot of us.

I had told Debbie on several occasions how much I admired her hosting skills and that I hoped to have a home like hers someday, a place where people would feel welcome. One day, she gave me a present: a beautiful silver serving platter that she had picked up at a garage sale. She said when she saw it she thought of me, and wanted me to have this for a time when I had a place of my own and could have people over. I liked it even better knowing it wasn't new—this was a dish that had seen service to others, something passed down. I still have it.

○   ○   ○

The concept of developing others and passing along the skills we've learned and the vision we've had is not only practical, it's biblical. For a long time Moses tried to do everything on his own. He stuck it out longer than most of us would have—he got to the point where he worked from sunup to sundown six days a week without a break. Eventually his strength gave out and he listened to the reason of his father-in-law, Jethro. He appointed others who were then able to deal with most of the initial problems before they even got to Moses. And slowly Joshua emerged more and more into the picture. He began as an aid to Moses, and later, when Moses needed someone to carry on the work, Joshua was there to lead the people into the Promised Land. The leadership was passed on. What might have happened if Joshua hadn't been prepared to carry on the work?

DO THIS

Engage with Scripture in your group by studying the spiritual gifts. After ensuring that everyone knows his or her gifts and has an outlet for using those gifts to serve others, go one step further: help people find a way to develop others in their area of giftedness.

WHO IS YOUR GRASSHOPPER?

Whatever we have learned, whatever gifts we have, we are responsible for helping develop these in others. If we are small group facilitators, we are called to develop other small group facilitators. But who? How do we know who to invest in? What qualities do we look for in a potential new leader? It's not always obvious.

One of the most commonly referenced passages in response to this question is 1 Timothy 3:1-13:

Here is a trustworthy saying: Whoever aspires to be an overseer de-

sires a noble task. Now the overseer is to be above reproach, faithful to his wife, temperate, self-controlled, respectable, hospitable, able to teach, not given to drunkenness, not violent but gentle, not quarrelsome, not a lover of money. He must manage his own family well and see that his children obey him, and he must do so in a manner worthy of full respect. (If anyone does not know how to manage his own family, how can he take care of God's church?) He must not be a recent convert, or he may become conceited and fall under the same judgment as the devil. He must also have a good reputation with outsiders, so that he will not fall into disgrace and into the devil's trap.

In the same way, deacons are to be worthy of respect, sincere, not indulging in much wine, and not pursuing dishonest gain. They must keep hold of the deep truths of the faith with a clear conscience. They must first be tested; and then if there is nothing against them, let them serve as deacons.

In the same way, the women are to be worthy of respect, not malicious talkers but temperate and trustworthy in everything.

A deacon must be faithful to his wife and must manage his children and his household well. Those who have served well gain an excellent standing and great assurance in their faith in Christ Jesus.

DO THIS

Ask others to take over areas of leadership responsibility in your small group. For example, designate one person as the party planner and another as the social-justice service coordinator.

TARA

WHEN I WAS A SMALL GROUPS PASTOR, I taught the leadership orientation for our church. One of the things I would do was have someone read this passage aloud. When the reading was finished, dead silence would ensue. Invariably, attendees at the leadership orientation were uncomfortable at this point. They began shifting in their seats, probably wondering why they had come. I asked people what they thought about the passage. Some brave soul would say that it was a bit hard to live up to, the standard seemed pretty high, and maybe no one should really aspire to be a leader. So then we'd talk about high standards. Yes, God does call us to something. It's not as if he's saying, "Do whatever you'd like—holiness is optional."

But then I asked them to name some of the prominent leaders in the Bible. And we looked at their lives. David. Peter. Moses. Paul. Hmm, not exactly paragons of virtue. Three out of four were murderers—and in Peter's case it isn't like it was for lack of trying (John 18:10-11). Yet God used them. David was a man after God's own heart. Peter (or his confession of Christ) was the rock upon which Christ would build his church. Moses was the only man God spoke to face-to-face, as a friend. Paul spread the gospel throughout Asia Minor.

○　○　○

So what are the qualities of a leader? When we look at the lives of biblical leaders, some striking qualities are humility, repentance, openness and change. These are people who, when their sin was pointed out, repented and were contrite.

It's not so much a matter of being perfect, but of how people deal with what is wrong. When we run across what is hidden in our lives, areas we're ashamed of, what do we do? Do we keep hiding it, or do we ask trusted friends for help?

So what do we look for in a potential leader for a small group? The Bible talks much more about character than about skills when it comes to leadership. Three qualities that can be distilled from 1 Timothy 3, as well as from biblical examples of leaders, are spiritual maturity, personal maturity, and teachability. If we start with these, the rest can be taught. Let's take a quick look at these three qualities:

Spiritual maturity. Spiritual maturity does not mean these leaders prayed the prayer to accept Christ a long time ago. Many people have done this and then done nothing spiritual since. It means a vibrant, living relationship with God—a relationship characterized by dedication to learning more about and from him.

There is no cast-iron rule about how long one must have been a Christian in order to lead, but we have examples in Acts of it having been much speedier than we might expect. Although sometimes it does take years, it doesn't necessarily have to. What's most necessary is having someone along to support new leaders, and perhaps even colead with them in the beginning before sending them off on their own. Like the "good and faithful servant" of Matthew 25:23, the key is to provide incremental opportunities for people to grow in leadership. You don't preach in front of large crowds before you lead small groups. And you don't lead small groups before you hand out bulletins at the door.

Personal maturity. This is just common sense, especially in leading small

DO THIS

Incremental leadership opportunities matter—for people at *all* levels of spiritual growth. Below is a partial list of small group tasks that could be delegated to someone else, either as a one-time task or as an ongoing responsibility.

• hosting group in their home

• bringing food

• welcoming new people

• planning a service project

• planning a social event

• organizing childcare

• incorporating art or music

• praying aloud

• facilitating the sharing time

• facilitating the discussion time

groups. Someone who can't get along with others or who has not worked on their own life and issues would not do well leading a small group. Personal issues not adequately dealt with will always—always— come up in a ministry position. Think of the senior pastor who cannot keep staff, the worship pastor who desperately needs to be liked, the children's pastor who alienates volunteers. Generally, these issues are not theological or spiritual in nature, but stem from personal issues. The same is true of small groups. Any personal issues will soon come to the fore and cause damage in the group.

Teachability. Arrogance stands as the enemy of biblical leadership. If you have any leadership books that wax eloquent about exuding confidence to impress others, do us all a favor and leave those at the door of the church before entering. Humility is required to learn, to lead others and to teach others to lead. If you sense arrogance in a small group leader or a pastor, run, and run now.

Once there was a young man, a seminary student, who began attending a local church. Within a few months of arriving, he offered to preach a sermon, stating that his giftedness was in the area of teaching. The senior pastor turned down his offer. A few weeks later, the nursery coordinator asked him if he would be willing to volunteer in the nursery. The seminary student declined, again stating that his gifts were in teaching. The tone of his response indicated that changing diapers was a bit beneath him.

Although in general, ministry should be done along the lines of giftedness, those who are unwilling to serve will be unfit to lead. Humility and teachability are essential qualities for those who exercise leadership in the kingdom of God.

One of the great myths of leadership is that all leaders look alike. Depending on the culture of the church, they all look like entrepreneurs, or they all look like scholars, or they all look like football heroes. In reality, there is no one trait all leaders share. Even within the area of small groups, different groups require different leaders.

We often look for the ready-made leader. Rather than merely looking for someone who has done it before, brainstorm qualities of the type of person you're looking for as an apprentice for your particular group. Remember that leading a group is a learning process. Personal and spiritual maturity and teachability are the most important things to start off with. The rest can be learned.

A WORD ON COACHING

Perhaps a bigger challenge than finding qualified potential facilitators is figuring out what to do with them after we've found them. How can we help them develop when we are still developing ourselves? Some helpful approaches to developing others include consulting, counseling, mentoring, discipling and spiritually directing—all of which are great options when they're available. But if your church is anything like ours, the people available to fill these roles are limited. Most people are in their twenties and thirties, resulting in a lot of people at similar levels of development. It's likely that the people in our small group we'll want to develop will be right around the same age we are. These dynamics lead to a great shortage of kung fu masters, at least in terms of age and experience.

But if we change the category to how people interact rather than how much age or experience they have, we can start getting somewhere. For this reason, much of our material is inspired by coaching—because coaching skills (such as discovering values, asking powerful questions and listening) can be applied effectively between people at similar life stages. Consulting, counseling, mentoring, discipling and spiritual direction require one person to be further along than the other. Although this may be true for the coach, it's not necessary. Coaching, in its purest form, relies on the approach to the conversation rather than the experience of the coach on the given topic.

The term *coaching* has become popular over the past decade. And as happens with most popular terms, it's often misused or incorrectly substituted to update words some communities don't want to use anymore, such as *mentoring* or *discipling*. In some communities these terms are synonymous with coaching. But it can be hard to differentiate between them when they function more as overlapping circles. Yet as the profession of coaching becomes more common, certain foundational principles have been established.

Coaching is a true partnership. Coaches listen, observe, believe and support. They are trained to see the image of God in others and to call forth their brilliance. Sounds a lot like the role of the kung fu master, doesn't it? They help people notice what's already there.

An assumption is that the answers dwell within a person. The coach's responsibility is to listen intently, to get curious about what they are hearing, and to ask questions to draw out those answers. Coaches don't offer advice unless it's requested.

An inherent respect for others, their stories and God's creativity in growing them leaves little room for the coaching relationship to be about the coach or coach's experiences. Listening takes place at levels You and Us.

Coaches are also trained to notice and name the limiting beliefs, false assumptions or draining perspectives that might be getting in the way of the other's progress—without trying to fix the person.

Certainly there is some overlap between coaching and discipling or mentoring, but the differences are significant as well.

As people develop, so much self-confidence is instilled when someone they respect is saying—either directly or indirectly—"I believe you have the answers." Sometimes people want our help and advice—that's true. But they *always* want to be heard, and they always want to know we think they can do it. We can serve as sounding boards for those we are developing as new facilitators by making use of coaching skills.

JENN

I REMEMBER A CONVERSATION I HAD with my older sister, Kecia, shortly after I started learning about coaching. She was sharing some facts with me about her job and a promotion she was interested in pursuing. Historically, in a conversation like this with Kecia, I would have started giving advice, and then she would have started getting frustrated. After all, who wants advice from their little sister? My temperament combined with my background in human resources sometimes get me in trouble here—so this time I tried something different. I started saying things like, "What do you think would be helpful for you to do next?" And, "That's a great idea! When are you going to do that?" Kecia lit up and came up with a great plan.

○   ○   ○

Coaching has the greatest impact when the coach believes in the other persons more than they believe in themselves—when the coach holds a larger vision for their life and ministry than they have. Seeing their uniqueness and giftedness and saying, "The world needs more of *that*." Helping them see that taking risks and trusting God may not always lead to success the way the world defines it, but that it always leads to growth and redemption.

DO THIS

Identify the strengths of the members of your small group. Outside of the group time, choose a couple of people to intentionally develop and encourage. Start by communicating that you believe in them as leaders and notice the effect it has.

Coaching is unique in this approach to development—this belief in the other, in the image of God in them and the giftedness God has placed in them, and in drawing out their own resources. This approach to developing others yields far better results and far more integrated people than trying to create cookie-cutter group leaders. Each facilitator has something different to offer. And that's good.

HOW DO WE ACTUALLY DEVELOP OTHERS?
SOME PRACTICAL ADVICE

Working ourselves out of a job is one of the best things we can do as small group leaders. After all, we will not be leading forever. All facilitators need to be able to take breaks, start different groups or make time for new ministries that will grow and stretch them. And to do that, we need to be able to delegate and develop others.

Show-how training. Bob Logan, who coaches church planters and other ministry leaders, has developed a very simple outline for developing others that he calls "show-how training." It's modeled from how Jesus taught his disciples. Although this outline can be helpful for teaching any number of skills, it's especially easy to apply to small group facilitation. Here are the steps:

- I do, you watch.
- I do, you help.

- You do, I help.
- You do, I watch.
- You do, someone else watches.

These steps are straight-forward and ensure that a person has the support they need without feeling in over their head. We've seen our pastor, Ron, use these steps effectively when developing a new communicator. When he notices someone who displays an undeveloped gift in this area, he might ask the person to help him brainstorm about an upcoming message series. If that goes well, Ron asks him or her to speak one week on a topic and coaches the person through developing the message. He accompanies the new speaker to the services and listens to the message. Eventually he might be comfortable having the new speaker fill in when he's out of town. Ron repeats each stage if necessary and offers feedback and coaching along the way.

DO THIS

Think of an area where you would like to grow. Seek someone outside your small group who you believe could help you develop in this area and ask him or her to lead you in show-how training.

The steps are the same when developing a small group facilitator, just in a different context. The regular facilitator may ask someone to meet outside of group to help plan some of the material. Then maybe the leader would ask that person to facilitate a twenty-minute segment of the group on a particular issue. They'd plan and debrief together along the way. Then maybe the new facilitator would take a whole evening while the regular leader observes.

Debrief regularly. As facilitators work through this basic outline to develop others, they'll need to meet together to debrief regularly. Even when it seems like that debrief time isn't needed, it is. One time Sylvia was leading a group, and she asked Kayla to facilitate one night. Kayla did, and the time went wonderfully. People seemed engaged, they were participating, the evening was productive and fun. Sylvia thought, *I probably don't really need to check in with Kayla—it's pretty obvious how well things went.* But she invited Kayla to get coffee that week anyway. When they met, Kayla launched in with an apology. She felt she'd done a poor job, that the group hadn't gone well at all, and that Sylvia was probably regretting asking her to facilitate. Sylvia was stunned. The debrief was obviously needed.

Generally, debrief times can consist of a few basic questions along the lines of, How did you feel about the time? What did you notice? What was strong? and What would you like to see different next time? (See appendix six for more on preparing and debriefing.) Again, much more time needs to be spent asking questions and listening rather than giving advice. Like the coach or kung fu master, a good facilitator helps people see. The facilitator helps others take notice of what they experience in the group, and helps them reflect on their own experience and observations.

Avoid the dependency trap. A healthy group is one that can continue on without the original leader. Just as a pastor-centered church isn't healthy, a leader-centered group isn't healthy. The more experienced and gifted the small group leaders are, the more likely they are to run into the dependency trap. A group begins to view the leader as their own personal "Bible Answer Man," the one who always knows the right thing to say in any situation. Tim, a strong leader with a lot of education and charisma, began to run into this issue in his group. He began to notice that whenever someone in the group said something very deep—or very controversial or very challenging—others would turn and look to him. They were waiting for him to respond.

Tim worked out a strategy. Next time that happened, he asked, "How does the group want to respond to that?" The onus was placed on the group to be a group. Tim provided a good rule of thumb for avoiding the dependency trap: Never do anything for a group that they can do for themselves.

Intentionality: Pass the torch. Take the following scenario: Jason, the facilitator, says to his group, "I've been leading for a while now and I'd like to take a break. Would any of you like to step up to facilitate?"

There is an awkward silence while the group members look at each other. Some of the people in the group have only been attending for a few weeks. Some are thinking, *Hmm, I might like to do that, but what if I say that and others in the group are disappointed? Maybe they don't think I should.* Others are thinking, *I'm certainly not qualified, but what if someone else volunteers who isn't a very good facilitator? I kind of like Jason, and I'm not sure who else could do as good of a job.* And another might think, *Surely if Jason thought I'd be good at this he would have asked me.* Finally, someone says, *I'll do it.*

What's wrong with this picture? What are some of the problems you could see surfacing? Potential responses include:

- Someone not qualified wants to lead.

- Someone feels called but is afraid and doesn't come forward.

- People feel unchosen.

- People feel pressured.

- People feel rejected or leaderless.

- A huge opportunity has been missed.

A better route is to think through who might make a good facilitator, then make it a point to ask that person about it outside of group. If the person is interested, their skills and calling have been validated. If they are not interested, it was a nice compliment. People almost invariably take such an exchange as a compliment. So it can't hurt to ask.

And there are different questions to ask: Do you want to move toward leading this group? is different from, Do you want to facilitate one night? and different again from, Would you be interested in coleading and facilitating part of the time? Options abound. But intentionality is indispensable in developing others.

Build in transition time. Don't you just love having changes sprung on you? People in your group probably dislike it as well. Generally speaking, it's inadvisable to announce a change in leadership or structure at the end of a group meeting and then have that change effective immediately. If at all possible, allow for transition time while the current facilitator is still leading and the new facilitator is helping. Let the group know the plan for transition well in advance. And then, when the official transition takes place, be intentional about again telling the group who will be taking on new responsibilities. This gradual and intentional approach provides the new facilitator with a better starting point and a position of legitimacy.

KNOW YOUR BAGGAGE

Once a facilitator has some specific people in mind to develop as small group leaders, one issue that will need to be worked through is what it means to be a leader or a facilitator. Many people have negative connotations associated with the term *leader*. Often part of developing others means helping them think through their definition of *group leader* or *facilitator* and some of the baggage they may carry along with that title. As mentioned earlier, some may resist the title because they feel it implies that they are or need to be so much further ahead of others in the group.

DO THIS

Facilitate a discussion on development in your group. Ask people to share stories of others who have invested in them. Encourage them to invest in others. Take note of those who hope to develop in areas where you have natural gifts.

Here are some of the more common perceptions of small group facilitators—all of these have potential pluses and minuses:

- The fabulous leader: I've gotta be brilliant, make insightful comments. I've gotta be fabulous, a persona. I lead through charisma.

- The professor: I must impress them with my fabulous knowledge and depth of scholarship. If I've not been to seminary, I probably won't qualify as a leader.

- The antileader: I'm just here to help. I don't have any knowledge or leadership to contribute. Whatever you guys think is fine by me.

- The can't-we-all-be-friends leader: I will do anything to make sure we all get along. We have no agenda or purpose. We are social. It feels more like a Super Bowl party than a small group.

- The entrepreneur: We will grow this group large. We will multiply, disciple and prosper. We are on a mission from God.

- The therapist: We are about emotional depth and bonding. I am here to help people and dig for what is most profound about our souls. We process our lives.

- The comedian: We will have fun. I am here to make sure of that. I will make light of deep comments. Tears make everyone uncomfortable, so I'll make sure we avoid them.

Now, each of these types of leaders has some positives, some benefits. The therapist is great at noticing the subtext and drawing people out. The can't-we-all-be-friends leader makes everyone feel warmly welcomed and included. But all of these options—in different ways—can make it more about the people than about God. Know your own defaults—and the defaults of those you're developing—and think through ways you can be intentional about shifting the focus to God.

Think through what kinds of roles may be needed at different times in the life of the group. The can't-we-all-be-friends leader may be much needed in the early stages when people don't know each other well and are afraid to go too deep too fast. But when people are ready to go deep, the therapist may be more helpful than the comedian.

THERE'S MORE THAN ONE WAY TO SPLIT A GROUP

I LEARNED HOW TO MULTIPLY A GROUP THE HARD WAY—I don't recommend trying this at home. When my husband and I led our first small group, it started out very, very small. For a couple of months only two guys were coming regularly. But slowly it grew, and eventually we looked around our living room and decided we were out of space. We usually had twelve to fifteen people showing up and it was a small apartment. People were starting to sit in the dining room and listen from there. We noticed people weren't talking as much as they used to—there just wasn't as much airtime per person. So Mark and I talked and decided the group should be multiplied into two groups. We called another couple who was attending and asked them to take half the people to their house. They agreed. Then we decided who should go where, based on a combination of geography and personality.

Mind you, we hadn't discussed any of this with the group yet.

We announced the plan the following week and—surprise, surprise—were met with immediate resistance. People voiced their dissent in the group, "But we all want to stay together!" "We'll miss the people who go with the other group!" "Maybe we should just find a bigger house to meet in." People also voiced their dissent by taking us aside, saying, "I can't believe you didn't talk with me about this." "I really want to be in the group with so-and-so." "I don't want to go to the group with so-and-so. He asked me out, I said no, and it would be really awkward. Can we be in separate groups?"

Slowly, we undid the damage. We eventually did pull off multiplying the group, but it was like pulling teeth. Not exactly the recommended method.

○   ○   ○

When a group grows too large to continue being effective, there are options. Below are four possibilities, but you can probably think of more.

Multiplication, but done well. The problem with Tara's story is not with the principle of multiplication but with the method—or lack thereof. Multiplication of groups, although it can be very difficult to make happen, can work very well if the whole group is involved in the conversation. The wise facilitator starts the group with that expectation in mind: "Eventually maybe this group will grow and become two groups with new leaders."

Then later the facilitator helps the group get in touch with the discomfort: "It's really getting crowded in here." "There's not much group time available to hear from each person." "Sharing is becoming less personal." "I notice we seem to have stopped inviting new people."

This last comment taps into issues of mission and vision. What are we about? What is the point of our group? What does it mean if we are moving away from being inclusive and inviting? The resulting conversation presents an opportunity for the group to define or redefine itself with an outward focus. For the group to continue reaching out to others and be inclusive and welcoming, it may need to multiply.

DO THIS

If you sense it might be time for your group to multiply, ask if some members would be willing to form a core group of people whose purpose is to create another small group in the future. Give members of that group opportunities to grow and develop their skills before the multiplication takes place.

Once the mission is agreed upon, logistics can be decided from there. And it's amazing how much more easily it's decided when people have been consulted beforehand and are on board with the idea of multiplying the group in the first place.

Closing the group. Almost inevitably when a group grows too large, someone will suggest closing it to new people. It's one of the first ideas to come to mind, as it presents a very simple, immediate solution. But only in some cases is closing the group the best option. Is the group trying to answer the question, How can we stop the growth? or How can the group best accomplish its intended purpose? The second question is more to the point. What is the purpose of the group? Then given that purpose, what might be the best solution?

If the purpose of the group is deep, intimate relationships, closing can be considered an option. (Even then, it may not be the best option. Twelve-step groups, where the core values require depth and honesty, are open groups.) If the purpose of the group is to develop leaders, then it may be helpful to close the group for a season, then send participants out to start new groups.

However, in most cases, the purpose of a small group is some combination of studying the Bible, growing in Christ, praying together, supporting one another, reaching out to newcomers and building community. In those cases, closing would actually be counterproductive.

Creating groups-within-a-group. One very social group thrived on including new people. It was often the first place newcomers to the church went to get connected. The group functioned as a gateway into the church; after people attended for a while and met some friends, they began to feel like they were a part of the core of the church. This group had a very important purpose. They also had a problem—they got too big.

Cindy, the facilitator, got creative. First she moved it to a larger venue. That worked for a while. Then she structured the time so there was a bit of teaching at the beginning to the whole group, then half the group went into one room and half went into the other room to discuss the teaching. That worked for a while too, but people started saying they were having a hard time getting to know others on a deeper level. Finally Cindy added prayer groups to the end of the meeting time: for the last twenty minutes people gathered in groups of three or four to pray in almost every room of the house. Eventually Cindy had to move on to the next option . . .

Branching off. Another way to start new groups is branching off. After all, large groups have one significant natural resource: lots of attenders who want to be part of a group. People who are interested in starting new groups can visit existing large groups, share a bit about the type of group they will be starting, and see if anyone wants to go along with them to start the new group. This approach is different than classic multiplication, since the group doesn't divide down the middle, but the new facilitator simply invites some willing group members to come along with the new group start.

Cases where branching off works especially well:

- When the new facilitator is known by the group. Often when new facilitators are raised up from within the existing group, they find they have little to no difficulty finding several people willing to go with them to start a new group.

- When the new group has a unique vision (e.g., a group that will focus on serving the poor, or that will do a series on dating, or that will major on prayer).

- When the new group meets in a different neighborhood or on a different night. If the time or location is more convenient for some of the people in the existing group, they'll be likely to make the change.

The beauty of branching off is that it's all voluntary. No one has to leave. No one is being forcibly separated from friends. Each person can choose for him- or herself. There's a lot to be said for not pulling teeth.

Whatever option is chosen, here are a few things to remember:

- Plan for growth. Growth is a natural result of health. Think through what might be some good options should the group grow too large.

- Regularly communicate the vision and purpose of the group. People need to be reminded at least once a month.

- When the group begins growing too large, involve them in the dialogue, allow everyone to have their say, and listen carefully. People's concerns need to be heard and their opinions need to matter.

- Think through all possible options with a focus on the purpose of the group. Which option will best allow the group to live out its purpose?

- When someone in the group seems to have a different vision for what the group is about, consider that God may be leading them to start a new group. Potential conflict can be turned into opportunity.

Sister group. Some small groups may be closed for the sake of depth of conversation and intimacy within the group. If those groups desire to develop community with a broader group of people, a sister-group option could be considered. A sister group is simply another small group within the same church with a similar purpose. Forming a sister-group relationship involves getting group members to agree and then finding a good match. Singles may want to mix more with families, for example, or a women's group may want to mix with a men's group.

One group of single men developed a desire to grow in their understanding of what it means to be godly men—including how it looks to cherish women. After studying and discussing the topic for some time, they decided to apply what they were learning. The group invited a women's group to a dinner that they had planned and prepared. They picked the women up, cooked the meal, created a nice ambiance and shared good conversation. They read poetry and listened to music, laughed and shed a few tears too. In this case the dinner party was a one-time event, but many sister groups have an ongoing relationship—the facilitators of each group intentionally organize joint events. In another case, two couples' groups decided to have dinner together quarterly to foster relationships and create additional support within the church.

Developing others requires effort, time, intentionality and investment. It requires counting the cost. Yet if we are conscious about developing and investing in others, our contribution goes far beyond teaching them facilitation skills. We are developing them as leaders and as persons. Our investment in them is a kingdom investment that goes far

WHEN THESE CHARACTERISTICS
DESCRIBE YOUR GROUP, IT'S TIME TO MULTIPLY:

- *More than twelve people attend regularly.*
- *The house is starting to feel crowded.*
- *Scheduling is becoming a problem.*
- *Two different ideas are emerging about group direction.*
- *Some groups members are driving too far to attend and participate fully.*
- *People are beginning to attend sporadically.*
- *Apprentice leaders are trained and functioning.*
- *Members hesitate to bring anyone new due to size.*
- *Leaders are feeling burned out.*

(From an online church planting course on www.coachnet.org.)

beyond any particular small group or church.

And we are usually surprised, time and again, at how being used by God becomes a blessing in and of itself, just as when we serve the poor and the outcast only to find that we are actually the ones being blessed more than them.

When we invest in another, we experience the sacred privilege of witnessing his or her growth. And it's uneven growth—like the cabin built by hand, the one with the fingerprints in the mortar and the off-center chimney. We were there when it was built. We have seen the cracks in the mortar—we know why they're there and we know at what cost they were patched. We know there are no true right angles in the entire house, and we've seen the marble placed on the floor roll around trying to find a level spot. But we've also seen the hand-carved woodwork on the staircase. And we know how the sunroom was designed so the light hits it just right for reading in the afternoon. We know how the fireplace stones were chosen and how much work went into placing them.

We know why Jacob walks with a limp—and we know why that's so much better than the way he walked before (see Genesis 32:24-32).

EXERCISES AND REFLECTION QUESTIONS

1. Read the following verses from Exodus 18 and reflect on the questions below.

> The next day Moses took his seat to serve as judge for the people, and they stood around him from morning till evening. When his father-in-law saw all that Moses was doing for the people, he said, "What is this you are doing for the people? Why do you alone sit as judge, while all these people stand around you from morning till evening?"
>
> Moses answered him, "Because the people come to me to seek God's will. Whenever they have a dispute, it is brought to me, and I decide between the parties and inform them of God's decrees and instructions."
>
> Moses' father-in-law replied, "What you are doing is not good. You and these people who come to you will only wear yourselves out. The work is too heavy for you; you cannot handle it alone. Listen now to me and I will give you some advice, and may God be with you.

You must be the people's representative before God and bring their disputes to him. Teach them his decrees and instructions, and show them the way they are to live and how they are to behave. But select capable men from all the people—men who fear God, trustworthy men who hate dishonest gain—and appoint them as officials over thousands, hundreds, fifties and tens. Have them serve as judges for the people at all times, but have them bring every difficult case to you; the simple cases they can decide themselves. That will make your load lighter, because they will share it with you. If you do this and God so commands, you will be able to stand the strain, and all these people will go home satisfied. (vv. 13-23)

- In what ways can you relate to the struggles Moses faced as a leader?

- Are you able to handle the work you are doing alone? Or is the work you are doing being done inefficiently?

- What is something you would like to delegate?

- Who is the godly person you believe is naturally wired to handle this responsibility?

2. Do you shy away from the label leader? What is keeping you from embracing this role in the kingdom of God?

3. Who has been involved in your development? And what did they do that really made a difference? How can you "pay it forward"?

4. Who has discouraged your development? What would you like to confess and forgive him or her for?

5. Look again at the passage from 1 Timothy 3 (p. 177). Is there anything you may need to discuss with your pastor? What is preventing you from doing this? Who will you talk to?

6. Think of someone you believe in more than he or she believes in him- or herself. Do something to encourage that person. Perhaps send a note of encouragement. What do you notice?

7. What are some unaddressed personal issues that you've seen sur-

facing in your ministry? Perhaps you always have to be right. Or you feel threatened by some of the personalities in your group. Or you are holding tightly to control. How do you believe God is using your ministry position to transform you? What do you want to let go of? What do you want to embrace?

8. Pick someone in your group and ask him or her to participate in "see-how" training with you. What did you enjoy about it? What still keeps you from enjoying developing others?

9. What type of leadership style resonates with you (see pp. 187-88)? Tell someone in your small group your default and ask that person to tell you when you have slipped into that mode. What patterns do you notice?

10. What are the next practical steps for you to take with your small group?

7

THE RIVER
WIDENING

Spiritual Transformation

For now we see through a glass,
darkly; but then face to face:
now I know in part; but then shall
I know even as also I am known.

1 Corinthians 13:12 KJV

What is the point of small groups? Really, with all of this time and effort invested, there should be a point, right? If you've read this far, you will probably not be surprised by our conclusion. The goal of a small group is not community or Bible learning or developing leaders or learning interpersonal skills or any number of other wonderful, important things that small groups do indeed help us accomplish. Those are all good and necessary goals, but they are secondary—they are not the central point. The point of a small group is *transformation.* The change of persons. Spiritual growth. Real movement toward Christ-like character. Deep change of the heart—an opening and stretching of that heart toward God.

We've all seen transformation. The conversion experience that marks significant life change. The alcoholic going into recovery that sticks. The healing and softening that forgiveness brings. The movement of someone's heart toward God over a long stretch of suffering. But we're often at a loss for words when describing how it happened. It was the movement of the Holy Spirit, certainly. It was a choice on the part of the individual. It was prayer. Sometimes circumstantial components play a part. But *how* did the transformation happen? And—the real underlying question—how can we replicate that experience? How can we make that happen for us, for others? There are no easy answers to that one.

JENN

I HAD JUST MOVED TO DENVER AND WAS APPROACHING my mid-thirties when discontent started to seep into my life. It felt like my career, family and country were imploding. I was having a hard time finding meaning in my work. I was single and losing hope of ever being married or having children. Fading dreams affected me in a variety of ways. Most notably, the things I often turned to for security were crumbling, and it left me feeling pretty anxious and dissatisfied.

Thankfully there was one bright part of my life at the time: the church I attended. After just a few months in a new city I felt like I was developing some good friendships in the small group I was attending. The relationships were a meaningful part of my life that year (and still are today). I shared a lot with my friends about my discontent and found that some of them also struggled with similar feelings—especially that our work was meaningless.

I grew closer and closer to God that year through these struggles and the influence of this church's leaders and the small group members. They taught me more about what it means to know God. They challenged me to reconcile a broken relationship in my family. They supported me when I went through counseling and later when I took a leave of absence from work to get away for a while and listen to God. My community was encouraging me to rethink some of my flawed perspectives on the character of God.

Through a series of events I decided it would be wise to get certified as a life coach because I wanted to enhance my résumé, make myself more marketable in a weak post-9/11 economy and make myself a better leader. As I sat through a workshop one weekend I found myself forming a new dream of someday starting a small business in coaching. I started sharing my vision with a few friends in my small group.

The small group facilitators selected *Entrepreneurs of Life* by Os Guinness as the book for the group to read during this time. One night we were reading an excerpt from John Cotton, a seventeenth-century minister, about what makes a calling warrantable. I looked at my friend Craig who sat beside me and whispered, "Do you think I have a warrantable calling?" He replied with a strong sense of authority, "Yes, I do."

Craig knew my story. He knew my struggles and he knew my strengths. He was familiar with my ideas and dreams. And I knew Craig's heart. I knew he wouldn't speak with such authority unless he truly believed God was calling me into a new career. This is the beauty of small groups. We're able to hear God's voice more clearly when we're in close spiritual community with others, when we are known by and know others.

That incident, along with several others, helped me make the decision to quit my job and start a small business—a decision that led to significant transformation in my life. I learned to find my security in God. Well, more frequently, anyway. And I experienced him providing for me rather than me providing for myself. I learned how insidious my independence was, and I learned a lot about how much I'd been depending on my own good performance to get ahead in life and earn favor with others. Most importantly, I grew to trust God more.

Transformation usually happens during the difficult times—the times when bad things happen to us or when we come face to face with the bad things we have done, or when we face difficult decisions that require us to change in order to move forward. It has been so since the beginning. Cain, having murdered his brother, cried out to God for mercy, and roamed the earth a marked man—the mark was a blessing and a curse at the same time. King David, confronted as an adulterer and murderer, Nathan's finger pointing at him, repented. A woman about to be stoned looked into the merciful eyes of Jesus. A prodigal son, expecting rejection and scorn, turned up the road to his father's house to see his father running toward him. Peter denied Christ three times and then, hearing the rooster crow, he dissolved into bitter weeping. Paul persecuted the righteous and observed the stoning of Stephen, then was struck by a light from heaven, blinded for three days and healed as the scales fell from his eyes.

DO THIS

Ask everyone in your small group to share a story about a dark season of his or her life and redemptive transformation that took place as a result. Read James 1:1-12 together and discuss it.

Without other people, it's easy to get bitter and angry rather than see opportunities for transformation. We need someone else to remind us. Imagine having a strong friendship with a couple in crisis and telling them, "If you work through this, you'll have more freedom and intimacy when you get to the other side." They can't see that now. All they can see is this miserable relationship that seems like it will go on forever as it currently is. They need reminders of the truth. And they need someone who will walk through it with them as the sometimes painful transformation takes hold.

RESHAPING THE RIVERBANKS

We've been using the metaphor of a river throughout this book. It works in many ways: our relationship with God is the ultimate water source for the river; questions and facilitation are the banks, providing some definition and boundaries; sometimes there are still places with undercurrents that require listening and paying attention; conflict is hitting rocks or going over waterfalls.

But what we're talking about here with transformation is a complete reshaping of the river. Sometimes in nature something upsets the natural flow—an act of God, it's often called. Something happens that causes the river to change its pace or shift direction. Or something causes swift erosion or a change in the terrain and the river never looks quite the same again. Some storms, some acts of God, leave a permanent mark on the river.

When those kinds of major shifts happen, it doesn't always look like it's going to be an improvement. Sometimes it looks like utter devastation. But eventually the land will be beautiful again—different, maybe, but beautiful.

The Colorado River once ran peacefully through the western United States. Then the plateau it was running over slowly began to rise. The river was forced to shift course. Eventually it branched into a few channels and began cutting through the raised land. Volcanic activity later deposited ash and lava through the area, damming the river in numerous places and forming large lakes. The landscape was changed forever and we were left with the Grand Canyon. Sometimes it takes a storm of some kind to create true transformation.

One facilitator had been through some serious trauma in his family relationships in the past. In his group, he created an exceptionally warm and inviting atmosphere. He exuded Fredrick Buechner's sentiment: "The party wouldn't be complete without you." His group, like most small groups, became an expression of him as a person. People, even those who were very new to the group, felt loved and accepted. How did he create such an environment? Partly through certain giftedness and wiring. Partly by the image of God shining through him. But mostly through his own time of difficulty and transformation, when he came face-to-face with his own failures and his own desire for love and acceptance.

Whatever transformation we've seen—or not seen—we bring with us to our groups. Our role as small group facilitators is not to create perfect small groups or perfect people. Quite the opposite. We're trying to create communities that can handle the imperfections of community and the people who attend. Places with enough cracks in the walls to let the light in. Because only the places with cracks allow transformation to come in.

WHAT CAN SMALL GROUPS DO TO AID TRANSFORMATION?

Transformation is our goal in small groups—yet at the same time it is something that is not up to us. God is the author of transformation. We cannot, by following certain steps or doing the right thing, bring about transformation in our own life or the lives of others. The most we can do is simply be open to it. To put ourselves—and our groups—in the best position possible for God to do his work.

What can small groups do to help bring about transformation? This is one of those times when it would be nice to have "five steps toward transformation" or a nifty acronym or, better yet, an acrostic of the word transformation—"T" is for "take time to reflect." But transformation cannot be wrapped up with a pretty bow. There's no formula. No way to plan for it.

Deep transformation is possible for people in small group community, but skills and spiritual maturity on the part of the facilitator are often the vehicles the Spirit chooses to use to get us there. Transformation is the end; skills are the bridge that helps us cross the chasm to get there. As facilitators, we develop skills and maturity to maintain openness to our own transformation and—potentially—to be used by God as an agent of transformation in the lives of others.

Given the lack of a formula, we cannot make transformation happen. We lack that power. But we can open the door and invite God in. So following are a few scattered thoughts about how facilitators can help their groups try to maintain a posture of openness to the transformation that God will bring about if and when he chooses. Skills and strategies are great for small group facilitators to have and use, but without a sincere openness to deep transformation, there's really not much point. So here are our thoughts—ways to try to maintain an openness to what God may be doing.

Engage in personal transformation.

- *Engage in our own transformation.* As facilitators, we need to notice how God may be speaking to us and to engage in our own transformational opportunities in order to take notice of the opportunities in the lives of others. Viewing transformation as an activity needed by others but not ourselves moves us into dangerous territory.

- *Spend time in prayer.* Since God is the sole source of transformation, we need to ask him to do his work in us. Prayer will help bring about a posture of openness, both individual and corporate.

- *Take time to reflect.* We don't often take the time necessary to be transformed in our culture—we have an inordinate fear of free time. Without taking the time to reflect on our experiences, it's unlikely we'll gain wisdom from those experiences, much less transformation. Small groups provide the somewhat unique opportunity in our culture as a place to process with a group of people rather than in isolation or one-on-one. They provide space for reflection—take advantage of that.

- *Be in deeper community with others.* Transformation rarely happens in isolation, but it's also less likely in a large group. It often takes a small community, an inner circle, to help us see what's going on in and around us.

Kent was struggling with trust in his marriage. He had been burned in his relationship with his ex-wife who had been unfaithful, and so this time around he came up with a strategy for protecting himself. Kent began trying to impose strict boundaries on his current marriage in order to feel safer, but those boundaries became increasingly restrictive and unhealthy. He sought to prevent any interaction between his wife and other men. Kent's wife became increasingly worried and felt as though he didn't trust her. Eventually she started pushing back on the boundaries he was trying to impose.

Kent confided in a close friend from their couples group. The friend

DO THIS

Schedule a day for a silent retreat with God. Ask him what he wants to reveal to you and how he would like to transform you. Be open and expect to hear from him. Encourage your small group to do the same.

calmly said, "I'm glad she's not putting up with your rules. Who would?" Kent was hoping to hear that he wasn't being unreasonable, she was. Instead what he heard was, "Who would put up with me?" Kent continued to ask himself this question. And he came to the same conclusion: No one. And he began to experience transformation. He was freed to love and trust more deeply, and he did.

Express the Spirit of Christ.

- *Show grace.* When a storm comes, it's a very different experience being shown grace instead of judgment. That's easy to say, but much harder to live out. Look back on your own life at your time of greatest failure and ask what it would have been like to have been shown grace at that point, and what it would have been like to have been shown judgment. What would have been different? Grace in the face of failure is one of the most powerful experiences of God that we'll ever experience.

- *Show faith in others.* Believe that God is at work in others' lives, even when you can't see it. Be patient and know that anything is possible. See yourself as one that walks alongside others rather than dragging them along like an unwilling donkey.

- *Be curious.* Listen carefully as you read Scripture, pray, engage in conversations and ask questions. What might God want to reveal of himself? Or what might he be revealing about ourselves that we need to see?

- *Show love.* Many people have experienced God in less-than-perfect small groups and in less-than-perfect churches, because love was shown. When a group cares about people and cares about God, God will show up.

Pam received an e-mail from an address she didn't recognize. But then she saw that it was from a woman who had attended a small group that Pam's father (now deceased) had facilitated when Pam was a child. The woman wrote that she joined his small group in 1980, very shortly after becoming a believer. She was writing to tell Pam how much Pam's father had influenced her, how her spiritual life evolved over the years, and how she'd made a recent decision to lead a small group with the hope that she could pass on that experience to someone else. She wrote, "I cannot tell you how much he stressed his love for all of us and how he carried us on his heart." Now that the woman has begun leading her own group, she wrote, "I can honestly say that I have a deep love for each one of these people. . . . Your father set an amazing example in that regard. And he left an amazing legacy."

DO THIS

Make a decision to extend grace (even if you don't necessarily feel grace) to someone in your community who has failed you or others. What is that person's response to your grace? What do you notice about the impact that extending grace has on you?

Cultivate awareness.

- *Become aware of opportunities for transformation.* There are certain times when we are more open to change and movement than usual. Sometimes it's during a major life crisis, a move or a breakup. Whatever the circumstance, be aware that sometimes those circumstances can propel us toward increased dependence on God. Watch for those opportunities and encourage people to engage with God as they weather the storm.

- *Stay in touch with our experience.* We can tap into our own transformational experience to help others. This does not mean shifting the focus to ourselves or our own experiences—for God often works in very different ways with different people—but simply being in touch with our own stories brings renewed empathy and understanding as we engage with others.

- *Be aware of our own sin.* An awareness of what we are capable of goes a long way. We all stand in need of grace and transformation. Pride does nothing but stand in the way. As facilitators, our modeling humility, honesty and awareness of our own sin will open the way for others to do so as well. The group is a reflection of the facilitator. If the group members hear the facilitator talking about his or her sin and struggles (not in generalities), they are more likely to regard the group as a safe place and open up about their own struggles.

J. J. had recently started attending a small group. Unlike many spiritual explorers who feel more comfortable hanging on the sidelines of churches and maintaining their anonymity, J. J. dove in on the deep end. After visiting one or two services, he began going to social events, service events and a small group. He built relationships and was up front about where he was at—a season of spiritual exploration. And he was checking out Christianity. J. J. had been through a recent breakup with his girlfriend and had just been laid off from his job. He sensed that a season of potential transformation was upon him and he was searching for it, actively opening himself up to God. He used his sudden extra time to read about world religions. He came to group with questions. One night, the group was spending some time in prayer, and for the first time since he'd started coming, J. J. prayed aloud. The presence of God hung thick in the room—everyone could feel it. J. J. was praying, telling God that he thought he believed now, that he wanted to go forward the next step, whatever that was. It was a step of faith, a moment of transformation.

DO THIS

Confess an area of sin to your small group. Discuss what it's like for you to struggle in this area and how it affects your leadership (e.g., causing you to feel like an imposter? Or unqualified for leadership?).

CREATING SPACE FOR GOD TO BE AT WORK

Remember that we cannot force transformation, either in ourselves or in others. As facilitators, it's not our job to make it happen in our groups. Transformation is up to God and requires the cooperation of the other person. We don't need to get too caught up in being great. Even if our group—or our facilitation, or our example—goes poorly sometimes, powerful things can happen if God is at work.

Transformation is all around us. It isn't always dramatic. But it always leaves its internal mark, the imprint of God having been at work. In small groups, we create a space for that to happen.

Ellie was part of a women's group. A single woman in her thirties, she very much wanted to be married. She felt called to be a wife and mother, but from where she sat right now, she couldn't see how that was going to happen. Then Ellie started dating a man who seemed wonderful—all she had been looking for. She fell head over heels for him within a couple of months. It wasn't until after she was emotionally invested that she started seeing red flags. As she processed the relationship with some trusted friends in the group, it became more and more apparent—to them and to her—that the relationship was not moving in healthy directions. Ellie knew she had a choice to make. After much prayer and wrestling with God, she broke off the relationship. It took every ounce of faith she had, and it felt more like a divorce than a breakup to her. Another season of deep transformation.

Mark was at Williams-Sonoma registering with his fiancée. He suggested that they register for a nice navy blue apron he was holding. She said it was black. He argued with her saying that clearly it was navy blue. He even grabbed a nearby black plate and held it next to the apron to show the difference in color. She said, "What's the tag say?" So he flipped the tag over and it said "solid black." Solid. How many tags say solid black on them? He was exposed. He started wondering why he always had to be right, so he took this question back to his men's small group. And he began to be transformed; that moment in Williams-Sonoma was the catalyst.

Elizabeth had struggled with an eating disorder in college. Even though she felt a long way from perfect health in this area, she recognized the growth that had taken place. She looked around the church and wondered where the women were going with their struggles around body image and eating. As Elizabeth built relationships with some of the women she met and shared parts of her own story, they opened up in turn. Just as she had suspected, unhealthy approaches to food and the body were just as much an issue inside the church as they were outside it. And most of the women felt they had no one they could talk with, not even their spouses. Elizabeth approached the small groups pastor and expressed a desire to start a support group. Wanting to be honest about her own struggles, she said, "I wonder about my qualification to lead this group. I still struggle with this and am certainly not 100 percent healthy. On the other hand, one of my best qualifications is that I understand. When women talk about the crazy things going on inside their heads—I get it." Elizabeth's willingness to use her imperfect story for the good of others resulted in a powerful group of women that engaged honestly at deep levels. And Elizabeth saw her experience redeemed as God used it in the lives of others. That's transformation.

GLORY REVEALED

As people created in the image of God, we are imprinted with his design. It's in us, maybe not fully realized, maybe not fully formed, but it's present. Someday, the image of God in us will shine out in all its fullness, unfettered by sin, shame or fear. But until then, we live in the in-between: the now and the not yet, as theologian George Ladd put it in his *Gospel of the Kingdom*. We wait for restoration of all that we once were and might one day be again. We wait with hope, with eager expectation, for the hand of God when in the darkness we cannot see him. We wait with snatched glimpses and tastes of what is to come. And in those glimpses and tastes we experience God and are transformed.

When the river comes finally to the ocean, having run its course, it opens up into the large delta plain. From there it runs into the ocean and is transformed. We are known, and we are connected to something bigger. It is no longer a river, but an ocean. A new thing. The transformation is complete.

> All streams flow into the sea,
>   yet the sea is never full.
> To the place the streams come from,
>   there they return again. (Ecclesiastes 1:7)

EXERCISES AND REFLECTION QUESTIONS

1. Read the following excerpt written by Annie Dillard and reflect on the questions below.

   > The secret of seeing, then, the pearl of great price. If I thought he could teach me to find it and keep it forever I would stagger barefoot across a hundred deserts after any lunatic at all. But although the pearl may be found, it may not be sought. The literature of illumination reveals this above all: although it comes to those who wait for it, it is always, even to the most practiced and adept, a gift and a total surprise. (from *Pilgrim at Tinker Creek*)

   - What are the links you make between this excerpt and transformation?

   - To what extent do you believe you can seek out transformation? And what is God's role in it?

   - What is the transformation you are waiting for?

2. As you read Romans 8:38-39 below, what are some of the things you notice that you fear may separate you from God?

   > For I am convinced that neither death nor life, neither angels nor demons, neither the present nor the future, nor any powers, neither height nor depth, nor anything else in all creation, will be able to separate us from the love of God that is in Christ Jesus our Lord.

3. What are your current sufferings? How do you imagine God will reveal his glory through these sufferings?

I consider that our present sufferings are not worth comparing with the glory that will be revealed in us. The creation waits in eager expectation for the children of God to be revealed. (Romans 8:18-19)

4. What are the doubts you have about being rooted in love? What doubts do you have about how wide, long, high and deep Christ's love is for you?

And I pray that you, being rooted and established in love, may have power, together with all the Lord's people, to grasp how wide and long and high and deep is the love of Christ, and to know this love that surpasses knowledge—that you may be filled to the measure of all the fullness of God. (Ephesians 3:17-19)

5. Learn more about spiritual disciplines. Which ones are you most drawn to? And how do you believe they may lead to transformation?

6. What are some of the most powerful stories of redemption you have read, watched in movies or experienced? What causes you to be so drawn to these stories of redemption?

7. Who are you becoming? Take time to reflect on how you hope that will affect you as a leader and believer.

Appendix 1

USING SCRIPTURE
IN SMALL GROUPS

Okay, I'll just say outright that my bias is for the Bible. As a small groups pastor, I was amazed at how many groups didn't want to study the Bible as their primary text. Many facilitators were afraid people wouldn't be drawn to their groups if they were seen as "Bible studies." Some were concerned that people in the group would find the material either too difficult or too boring. It just isn't true! Scripture has some of the most amazing stories you'll ever read. If a small group discussion around Scripture is done well, using open-ended questions and bringing a bit of imagination to the text, it's anything but boring. Some parts of the Bible may be hard to know what to do with, but dive in anyway and discuss them. God is up to our questions. Bring them to the text. Wrestle with them before God and others. Asking questions of the Scripture is one of the best ways of engaging with and learning the Bible.

One of the most rewarding groups I ever led was a plain old Bible study. We connected with each other beforehand and prayed at the end and did social events outside of group, but our discussion time consisted of reading a Scripture passage aloud, asking questions and dialoguing. Advantages? No one had reading or homework to do—or not do. And I only spent about twenty minutes a week in actual preparation for the discussion—I read the passage and came up with some open-ended questions. And we had great discussions. Whatever you do, don't over-prepare and try to be the Scripture expert. Rely on the people in the group to do some of the work of engaging with the text. After all, this is about their growth too.

If you don't have time for preparation or aren't confident forming your own questions based on Scripture, there are plenty of booklet-style discussion guides on books of the Bible, including many excellent options by our very own publisher, InterVarsity Press. We've also created some downloadable studies and put them on our website: www.findingtheflow.org. These guides have open-ended questions already there for you, and you can pick and choose among them as you like. Buy only one copy of the guide and ask them like they're your own—this approach avoids the "question, answer, question, answer" routine as people read ahead to the next question.

A group of mothers of young children wanted to study the Bible but wanted to do so in a more contemplative way. They also admitted they weren't going to do any homework whatsoever—not even the facilitator. *Lectio divina* was a great approach for them. It consists of four out-loud readings of the same Scripture passage. On the first reading, just listen for the content of the passage. On the second reading, reflect on the passage as it applies to your own life, paying attention to whatever words or phrases stand out to you personally. On the third reading, respond to God, dialoguing with him about the passage. On the fourth reading, simply listen to God, inviting him to speak through this passage and being open to whatever he might have to say.

If you absolutely must do a book study instead of the Bible, choose something substantive. C. S. Lewis and N. T. Wright require a bit of effort on the part of the reader, but they're well worth it. *Devotional Classics* is also a good collection of essay-length writings by significant Christians through history. The writers come from many different vantage points and traditions, so you may disagree with points here and there, but that's part of the fun and adds interest to the discussion. For a list of other books that we think can make good small group studies, go to our website at www.findingtheflow.org. But try the Bible first. You may be surprised at how well a small group can do by simply going to the Scripture, reading it aloud and asking questions about it.

Appendix 2

EXAMPLES OF PERSONAL VALUES

Accomplishment/Result

Achievement

Action/Progress

Adventure/Excitement

Aesthetics/Beauty

Altruism

Autonomy

Clarity

Commitment

Competition

Completion

Connecting/Bonding

Creativity

Emotional Health

Environment

Faith

Freedom

Honesty

Financial Freedom

Fun

Goodness/Integrity

Humility

Humor

Intimacy

Joy

Kindness

Leadership

Love

Loyalty

Mastery/Excellence

Openness
Orderliness/Accuracy
Nature
Partnership
Patience
Peace
Personal Growth/Learning
Planning
Power
Privacy/Solitude
Recognition/Acknowledgment
Risk-taking

Romance/Magic
Security
Self-control
Self-expression
Service/Contribution
Spirituality
Spontaneity
Trust
Visionary
Vitality
Wisdom

Appendix 3

SMALL GROUP
VALUES CLARIFICATION

To begin this exercise, cut up the values cards in this appendix.

1. Lay out the heading cards from left to right in the following order:
   Always Valued, Often Valued, Sometimes Valued, Rarely Valued, and
   Never Valued. Use the values heading below to help you.

2. Read the description on each value card and place it under the heading that best suits you. This is a forced distribution exercise, so not
   all values can be equally rated. You may only place as many values
   under each heading as indicated (5 always valued; 8 often valued; 16
   sometimes valued; 8 rarely valued; 5 never valued).

3. Record your values on the Values List for future reference.

Always valued (5)	Often valued (8)	Sometimes valued (16)	Rarely valued (8)	Never valued (5)

VALUE CARDS

Accountability Sharing in life's struggles and holding each other to higher standards	**Addressing tough issues** Facing issues with courage knowing that conflict results in growth	**Admitting failure** Humbly sharing weaknesses with each other
Advance planning Knowing what the plan is ahead of time; putting structure in place	**Asking forgiveness** Humbly seeking out those you have wronged	**Autonomy** Independence in planning, implementing and thinking
Being believed in Knowing that others feel confident about your capabilities and potential	**Believing in others** Feeling confident about others' capabilities and potential	**Challenging one another** Pushing people toward change in thoughts or actions
Confronting others Addressing sensitive situations	**Developing leaders** Taking time to invest in potential leaders	**Efficient use of time** Getting down to business; avoiding non-essential topics
Emotional depth Getting beneath the surface	**Ensuring smooth flow** Being prepared with an outline	**Excitement** Engaging in the thrill of a moment
Feeling equipped/ready Gaining the knowledge, wisdom and experience	**Forgiveness** Accepting and extending the blood of Jesus in exchange for sin	**Freedom of expression** Having permission to be real
Grace Offering what has not been earned	**Holding to the agenda** Sticking with the original plan	**Intellectual depth** Exploring theory and concepts; challenging opinions
Intimacy Heart-felt connection emotionally, spiritually, intellectually	**Involvement of the Spirit** Working with what shows up	**Large numbers** The more the merrier
Life change Experiencing growth in choices and behavior	**Momentum** Following the energy	**Openness** Sharing personal stories and struggles
Powerful moments Experiencing unexpected breakthroughs	**Purity** Committing to living a holy life	**Quality** Choosing to put forth the extra effort required to be exceptional
Reconciliation Working through difficult situations for the sake of a relationship	**Redemption** Restoring the honor, worth or value of someone or something	**Relationship** Meaningful connection to another person

VALUE CARDS (continued)

Respecting others Valuing people and their opinions	Risk Exposing oneself to a chance of mistake or failure	Sense of humor Inducing laughter and amusement
Serving others Sacrificing time and other resources for the sake of others	Social opportunities Seeking ways to improve the community or lives of others	Speaking truth in love Saying what you believe another may need to hear
Vulnerability Taking emotional risks	Willingness to go with the flow Trusting the group to carry the discussion	Other?

VALUES LIST

Always Valued (5)
1.
2.
3.
4.
5.
Often Valued (8)
1.
2.
3.
4.
5.
6.
7.
8.
Sometimes Valued (16)
1.
2.
3.
4.
5.
6.
7.
8.
9.
10.

VALUES LIST (continued)

11.	
12.	
13.	
14.	
15.	
16.	
Rarely Valued (8)	
1.	
2.	
3.	
4.	
5.	
6.	
7.	
8.	
Never Valued (5)	
1.	
2.	
3.	
4.	
5.	

Appendix 4

LIST OF
EMOTIONS

Acceptance	Envy
Affection	Euphoria
Aggression	**Fear**
Ambivalence	Forgiveness
Anger	Frustration
Anxiety	Gratitude
Apathy	Grief
Compassion	Guilt
Confusion	**Happiness**/Joy
Contempt	Hatred
Depression	Homesickness
Disgust	Hope
Doubt	Horror
Ecstasy	Hostility
Embarrassment	Hysteria
Empathy	Loneliness

Love   Remorse
Paranoia   **Sadness**
Pity   Shame
Pleasure   Suffering
Pride   Surprise
Rage   Sympathy
Regret

This list is taken from Wikipedia: Emotions <http://en.wikipedia.org/ wiki/-Emotions>. There is disparity among the experts about the main emotions. Psychologist Paul Ekman's list of five main emotions are in bold in the list above.

Appendix 5

TOOLS FOR HANDLING CONFLICT

Between me & group member	Between me & cofacilitator	Between two group members (if it's interfering with the group)
Try to determine where the conflict is on the stages of escalation (page 145)	Try to determine where the conflict is on the stages of escalation (page 145)	Try to determine where the conflict is on the stages of escalation (page 145)
Determine what your default conflict style is and what conflict style would be most appropriate for the situation (pages 154-55)	Acknowledge the conflict with the cofacilitator and that you want to get together to try to resolve it	Acknowledge the conflict with the group members and ask them to get together to try to resolve it with you mediating

Between me & group member	Between me & cofacilitator	Between two group members (if it's interfering with the group)
Develop a plan for addressing the conflict and create a dialogue using the feedback model (page 160)	With your cofacilitator, determine what your default conflict styles are and what conflict style would be most appropriate for the situation (pages 154-55)	Have them determine what their default conflict styles are and what conflict style would be most appropriate for the situation (e-mail them the descriptions)
Schedule time to meet with the person in a place that's quiet, private and fosters open communication; let them know you sense there is a conflict and that you want to get together to try to resolve it	Develop a plan for addressing the conflict, create a dialogue using the feedback model, and ask your cofacilitator to do the same (page 160)	Ask them to prepare for addressing the conflict and to create a dialogue using the feedback model (e-mail them the description)
Open the meeting with prayer and, using the steps outlined in feedback model for a conversation framework, engage in the dialogue you planned NOTE: At this step you may wish to introduce the feedback model to the other person and ask them to stay within the framework	Schedule time to meet with the other in a place that's quiet, private and fosters open communication	Schedule time to meet with them in a place that's quiet, private and fosters open communication
Evaluate (on your own) how the conflict went using the stages of escalation. Did you move back in the stages of escalation?	Open the meeting with prayer and, using the steps outlined in feedback model for a conversation framework, engage in dialogue	Open the meeting with prayer and then describe the stages of escalation and let them know you intend to try to help them move back a stage or stages

Between me & group member	Between me & cofacilitator	Between two group members (if it's interfering with the group)
If the conflict remains unresolved, refer to Matthew 18 to determine next steps	Evaluate (on your own) how the conflict went using the stages of escalation. Did you move back in the stages of escalation?	Using the steps outlined in the feedback model for a conversation framework, have them engage in dialogue by having one person complete steps one and two and then switching before moving to steps three and four *NOTE:* It's important to make sure they both acknowledge the need they have that's not being met by the other (stages of escalation)
	Follow up with the cofacilitator to see if he or she agrees that the conflict has de-escalated	Evaluate (with them) how the conflict went using the stages of escalation. Did the conflict de-escalate?
	If the conflict remains unresolved, refer to Matthew 18 to determine next steps	If the conflict remains unresolved, refer to Matthew 18 to determine next steps

Appendix 6

PREPARING AND DEBRIEFING

Before group, ask yourself:

- Where do you feel the Holy Spirit leading?
- What are the desired outcomes for the group's time together?
- How will the group achieve the desired outcomes?
- What powerful questions could be asked?
- What direction do you see the discussion going tonight?

After group, ask yourself:

- How did you sense the Holy Spirit moving in the group?
- What does this group value?
- What stage is the group in?
- What do we need in order to move to the next stage?
- Which questions were powerful?
- What was happening during times of Level Us listening?

- Was I asking or telling?
- Who is my apprentice?
- Is the group at its ideal size?
- Are there any unresolved conflicts?

Appendix 7

USING
THIS BOOK IN
FACILITATOR TRAINING

Although this book is geared toward anyone facilitating a small group, we've included downloadable PowerPoint training material for pastors who want to train and develop their small group facilitators. After all, training the facilitators in our own church was the initial objective in developing this material. We wrote the PowerPoint material before the book.

To download this PowerPoint presentation, go to www.ivpress.com/extras/findingtheflow. We have made it available at this address for purchasers of this book to use in their training sessions. (Please don't circulate this material to others.) You'll also see the accompanying handouts for participants.

WHO

This material was designed primarily for small group leaders in local churches or parachurch ministries. The experiential, dialogue-based approach allows it to speak simultaneously to those who are new to facilitating groups as well as those who have been doing it for years.

However, people who have taken the training have also found the material helpful for leading teams in the workplace and for navigating relationships. We recommend not just offering it to new and existing small group leaders, but opening it up to anyone who is interested in attending. The following statement is the announcement we put in our church program:

> Finding the Flow facilitator training: Do you facilitate small group discussions, either formally or informally? Would you like to dialogue with others and engage in practical exercises to sharpen your skills? Come to the Pathways facilitator training: Finding the Flow. We'll be covering topics such as asking good questions, listening, and general facilitation tips. Whether you lead a Pathways group, desire to lead a group, or facilitate discussions in your workplace setting, this training will address many of the critical points of leading groups well.

Opening up the training to a variety of people with unique perspectives added a great deal of value to the discussion.

WHAT

When you download the material, you'll see a PowerPoint presentation broken into seven sections corresponding to the seven chapters of this book. You'll also see handouts that can be printed, copied and distributed to those who attend your trainings.

WHEN

This course was designed "café" style—just tell your facilitators when you'll be going through which sections.

A few good options include

- seven Wednesday nights in a row
- two or three Saturday morning workshops
- a weekend retreat

The seven sections can be done in any order. Sometimes it's helpful to start with those topics that have the most immediate relevance to your small groups ministry.

HOW

One of the great benefits of the PowerPoint format is that you are the "face" of the training. This flexibility allows the material to be customized to the language and style your facilitators are familiar with. If we videotaped ourselves making a presentation, we might say "Holy Spirit" instead of "Holy Ghost," like your church does. Then you'd have to apologize for our being outsiders who don't know the correct lingo.

We also have tried to cut lengthy sections of explanation anyway to leave more room for exercises and dialogue—that's the important stuff, not the talking head. As you'll see under the notes section embedded in the PowerPoint, we've just placed a few lines of instructions in here and there that you can use to talk people through the training. It's far from a script.

The training can be adapted to groups of various sizes. If you have a group that is larger than ten, have participants make their introductions in groups of four or five, then do all exercises in those groups so people have enough time and space to interact and engage in dialogue.

TRAINING IS JUST THE BEGINNING

No matter how helpful training material may be—and we sure hope this is helpful—remember that it's only the beginning. People who are facilitating small groups are going to need relational support, troubleshooting and problem-solving, development, encouragement, and appreciation. All those relational pieces need to happen at the interpersonal level. We've included some ideas below for building those relational components into your small groups ministry on a larger scale. The specifics are examples that worked well in our church. They may or may not work in yours, so feel free to adapt them. Maybe instead of taking your facilitators to a concert in the park, you'd want to organize an outing to the monster truck races. To each his own. That's the beauty of the body of Christ. Hopefully the ideas below will serve as launching points for further thought.

1. Provide a contact person for every facilitator. This contact person— whether a pastor, a staff person, a lay coach or a mentor—should be in regular contact with the facilitator to provide support along the way. Most churches call this coaching, but it can be called anything, as long as relational and strategic support is consistently provided for each facilitator.

2. Provide opportunities for facilitators to connect with one another. Due to the social nature of groups, most facilitators end up hanging out with people in their own groups. And that's great, but it would be helpful for them to get to know the other facilitators as well. If your church is large, they may not even know who the other facilitators are. At Pathways, we held "facilitator dinners" quarterly. (And we actually stole this idea from Cherry Hills Community Church in Highlands Ranch, Colorado, so it's not original with us either.) Facilitator dinners consist of four to six facilitators getting together with the small groups pastor over dinner to talk about how the groups are going. (If the church is larger, coaches can facilitate these dinners, or the pastor can spread the dinners throughout the year, so he or she attends one each week or each month, while each facilitator attends one quarterly.) The exchange of ideas and mutual encouragement at these dinners is wonderful. Don't try to blend these times with training; allow the relational component to reign supreme. Give each facilitator a bit of time in the spotlight, and together they'll end up talking about what needs to be discussed. And don't forget to spend some significant time in prayer together.

3. Develop your facilitators. Invite your facilitators to hear a speaker who's coming into town. Let them attend the spiritual-formation retreat free. Buy them a book. E-mail them a link. Help them find ways to continue to grow and develop, as a facilitator and as a person.

4. Encourage your facilitators. Send each facilitator a handwritten note or a Christmas card. Give the facilitators a call to see how they're doing. Take the time to ask questions and listen.

5. Celebrate with your facilitators. Build in times for having fun. Invite all the facilitators to go out to a baseball game together. Have a cookout at your house. Organize a concert in the park. In Denver they have several free concerts in parks during the summer—making for one of our least-expensive leader appreciation events ever.

BIBLIOGRAPHY

Bonhoeffer, Dietrich. *Life Together.* New York: HarperOne, 2003.

Csikszentmihalyi, Mihaly. *Flow: The Psychology of Optimal Experience.* New York: Harper & Row, 1990.

Dear, John. *The Questions of Jesus: Challenging Ourselves to Discover Life's Great Answers.* New York: Image, 2004.

Dillard, Annie. *Pilgrim at Tinker Creek.* New York: Harpers Magazine Press, 1974.

Donahue, William. *Managing Interpersonal Conflict.* Thousand Oaks, Calif.: Sage, 1992.

Enger, Leif. *Peace Like a River.* New York: Atlantic Monthly Press, 2002.

Goleman, Daniel. *Emotional Intelligence: Why It Can Matter More Than IQ.* New York: Bantam, 1995.

Goleman, Daniel, Richard E. Boyatzis and Annie McKee. *Primal Leadership: Learning to Lead with Emotional Intelligence.* Cambridge, Mass.: Harvard Business School Press, 2004.

Gottman, John M. *Why Marriages Succeed or Fail: And How You Can Make Yours Last.* New York: Simon & Schuster, 1995.

Guinness, Os. *Entrepreneurs of Life*. Colorado Springs: Navpress, 2001.

Ladd, George Eldon. *Gospel of the Kingdom*. Grand Rapids: Eerdmans, 1959.

Logan, Robert E., and Sherilyn Carlton. *Coaching 101*. Saint Charles, Ill.: ChurchSmart Resources, 2003.

Love, Patricia, and Steven Stosney. *How to Improve Your Marriage Without Talking About It: Finding Love Beyond Words*. New York: Broadway, 2007.

McNeal, Reggie. *Revolution in Leadership*. Nashville: Abingdon, 1998.

O'Rourke, P. J. *Holidays in Hell*. Jackson, Tenn.: Grove Press, 2000.

Putnam, Robert. *Bowling Alone*. New York: Simon & Schuster, 2001.

Robinson, Marilynne. *Gilead*. New York: Farrar, Straus & Giroux, 2004.

Steinbeck, John. *The Grapes of Wrath*. New York: Viking Press, 1939.

Thomas, Kenneth W., and Ralph H. Kilmann. *Thomas-Kilmann Conflict Mode Instrument*. Tuxedo N.Y.: Xicom, 1974.

Tuckman, Bruce W., and Mary Ann C. Jensen. *Stages of Small Group Development*. Thousand Oaks, Calif.: Sage, 1977.

Weeks, Dudley. *The Eight Essential Steps to Conflict Resolution*. New York: Tarcher, 1994.

Wheatley, Margaret J. *Finding Our Way: Leadership for Uncertain Times*. San Francisco: Berrett-Koehler, 2007.

Whitworth, Laura, Henry Kimsey-House and Phil Sandahl. *Co-Active Coaching: New Skills for Coaching People Toward Success in Work and Life*. Mountain View, Calif.: Davies-Black, 1998.

Whyte, David. 2006. "Thought Leaders: David Whyte on Courageous Conversation." Interview by Karen Elmhirst. HR.com, January 18.

Woolf, Virgina. *To the Lighthouse*. New York: Harcourt, 1927.

ADDITIONAL
RESOURCES

THE WATER SOURCE

Knowing Yourself

Brueggemann, Walter. *Spirituality of the Psalms.* Minneapolis: Augsburg Fortress, 2001.

Buckingham, Marcus. *Trombone Player Wanted.* 90 minutes. The Marcus Buckingham Company, 2006. DVD.

Goleman, Daniel, Richard Boyatzis and Annie McKee. *Primal Leadership: Learning to Lead with Emotional Intelligence.* Boston: Harvard Business School Press, 2002.

Hagberg, Janet O., and Robert A. Guelich. *The Critical Journey.* Salem, Wis.: Sheffield Publishing, 1995.

Keirsey, David. *Please Understand Me II: Temperament, Character, Intelligence.* Del Mar, Calif.: Prometheus Nemesis Books, 1998.

Myer, Isabel Briggs. *Gifts Differing: Understanding Personality Type.* Mountain View, Calif.: Davies-Black, 1995.

Rath, Thomas. *StrengthsFinder 2.0: A New and Upgraded Edition of the Online Test from Gallup's Now, Discover Your Strengths.* New York: Gallup Press, 2007.

Rohr, Richard. *The Enneagram: A Christian Perspective.* Crossroad General Interest, 2001.

Schwarz, Christian A. *The Threefold Art of Experiencing God.* Saint Charles, Ill.: ChurchSmart Resources, 1999.

Scazzero, Peter, and Warren Bird. *The Emotionally Healthy Church: A Strategy for Discipleship that Actually Changes Lives.* Grand Rapids: Zondervan, 2003.

Wagner, C. Peter. *Discover Your Spiritual Gifts.* Ventura, Calif.: Regal Books, 2002.

Zimmerman, F. Benedict, ed. *Interior Castle or The Mansions.* White-fish, Mont.: Kessinger, 2003.

CHARTING THE COURSE

Stages of Group Life

Bonhoeffer, Dietrich. *Life Together.* San Francisco: HarperSanFran-cisco, 1954.

Cloud, Henry, and John Townsend. *Boundaries: When to Say Yes, When to Say No to Take Control of Your Life.* Grand Rapids: Zondervan, 1992.

Myers, Joseph. *Organic Community: Creating a Place Where People Natu-rally Connect.* Grand Rapids: Baker Books, 2007.

EXPLORING THE UNDERCURRENTS

Listening to God and Others

Hybels, Bill. *Too Busy Not to Pray: Slowing Down to Be with God.* Down-ers Grove, Ill.: InterVarsity Press, 1998.

Wheatley, Margaret J. *Finding Our Way: Leadership for an Uncertain Time.* San Francisco: Berrett-Koehler Publishers, 2005.

Willard, Dallas. *Hearing God: Developing a Conversational Relationship with God.* Downers Grove, Ill.: InterVarsity Pres, 1984.

STIRRING THE WATERS

Asking Good Questions
Miller, Linda J., and Chad W. Hall, *Coaching for Christian Leaders: A Practical Guide*. St. Louis, Mo.: Chalice Press, 2007.

Gempf, Conrad. *Jesus Asked*. Grand Rapids: Zondervan, 2003.

ROCKS IN THE RIVERBED

Navigating Group Conflict
Ury, William L. *The Third Side: Why We Fight and How We Can Stop*. New York: Penguin Books, 1999.

Weeks, Dudley. *The Eight Essential Steps to Conflict Resolution*. New York: Tarcher, 1994.

CREATING NEW STREAMS

Developing New Leaders
Logan, Robert E., and Tara Miller. *From Followers to Leaders*. St. Charles, Ill.: ChurchSmart Resources, 2008.

Ogden, Greg. *Transforming Discipleship: Making Disciples a Few at a Time*. Downers Grove, Ill.: InterVarsity Press, 2003.

Whitworth, Laura, Henry Kimsey-House and Phil Sandahl. *Co-Active Coaching: New Skills for Coaching People Toward Success in Work and Life*. Palo Alto, Calif.: Davies-Black, 1998.

THE RIVER WIDENING

Spiritual Transformation
Calhoun, Adele Ahlberg. *Spiritual Disciplines Handbook: Practices That Transform Us*. Downers Grove, Ill.: InterVarsity Press, 2005.

Cloud, Henry. *Integrity: The Courage to Meet the Demands of Reality*. New York: HarperCollins, 2006.

McNeal, Reggie. *A Work of Heart: Understanding How God Shapes Spiritual Leaders*. San Francisco: Jossey-Bass, 2000.

FLoW

CONVERSATIONS
THAT MOVE

For more help and information or to connect with the authors,
visit www.findingtheflow.org.